D1414470

RECLAIMING EDEN

Taming the Serpent Ego

Daniel D. Schroeder

PUBLISHED BY WESTVIEW, INC., NASHVILLE, TENNESSEE

ISBN 978-1-935271-33-8

First Edition, October 2009

Printed in the United States of America on acid free paper.

RECLAIMING EDEN

Taming the Serpent Ego

Table of Contents

To Alice, Mary and Nikki

Three generations of angels in my life

INTRODUCTION

The story of the garden of Eden is one of the most ancient and well-known stories of all time. Or is it?

Do we have a true understanding of this story? Is it possible that there is something deeper in its words? Perhaps it's time to take a fresh look at Eden and see that its imagery can offer us some new understanding into our lives, our purpose, and our relationship with God. After you have walked through the pages of this book, you, too, may realize that the gate to the garden of Eden was never really blocked at all, but is waiting for us to return.

The images that come to mind when we think of the garden of Eden are those that have been formed in our minds from the numerous times we heard this story. The first man and the first woman were placed in the garden to tend it, to walk among the plants and animals, and to enjoy the beauty of the presence of God. Things were going fine until the serpent confronts Eve who yields to its temptation and eats of the forbidden fruit. She then shares this fruit with Adam. Eventually, God finds out about it and casts them from the garden in their now fallen state.

The Eden story has been used to explain original sin, sexual temptation, sexual maturation, the existence and scariness of snakes in the world, pain during childbirth, and our struggles working the earth for food. St. Paul uses this story to explain how sin came to be: "sin came into the world through one man, and death came through sin, and so death spread to all because all have sinned..." (Romans 5:12) He positions Christ as the remedy to this by adding, "For as all die in Adam, so all will be made alive in Christ." (I Corinthians 15:22)

Despite the various interpretations offered about the Eden story, it's true that we all have a serpent to face in our lives. In fact, this serpent is the very same one that Eve encountered in the garden of Eden. This is a serpent that would gladly run our lives for us so that we no longer have to think or feel or, for that matter, even know that we're alive. It will lull us each into a sleep that casts a veil over our true self, over the person whom God created each of us to be, but who has now been lost in the falsehood of a dysfunctional ego otherwise known as the serpent.

I invite you to join me in the most important journey of our lives. It's a journey from the darkness of a false sleep to the light of full awareness. It's a journey to discover who we were meant to be; a journey to heal ourselves of the wounds of the past and the fears of the future; a journey to fully realize the spiritual birthright God wishes to bestow upon us. By taking this journey, we may discover how to be fully alive. This is the journey of our salvation.

This book can be viewed as one of the stepping stones across a river that separates us from a state of awareness, or enlightenment. This river contains the fast-moving forces of a dysfunctional culture and society that would have us remain on this side, where we can be controlled and manipulated. Within these waters swims the sly serpent, guarding against any attempt at crossing over to the other bank. The other side, however, is where our true destiny lies, a place of truth, unity, and understanding; a land where we're all interdependent and live lives that we were meant to live; a place where God is glorified because we're complete.

Using selected verses of the first three chapters in the book of Genesis as our foundation, we'll arm ourselves with the basic tools needed for this journey. Of course, we must be motivated to begin the journey, to abandon our current state of 'spiritual sleep', and enter what is really our natural state. Some people may not want to cross the river. Others may not even know that the river exists. Still others will doubt that life is better on the other side, and some may have heard stories about how dangerous it is to cross. "What if I get lost?" "What if I slip and drown?" "How can we get back if we don't like it over there?" "I'm not good enough to be over there." All these whisperings of the serpent will keep us locked in its grip, on this side of the river. If this journey does not make sense to you, then this book will not make sense either. Set it aside for now and wait until you are prompted once again to consider the journey.

Those ready to begin the journey will find within these pages what they need to take the first step. And for those of you who have already tried to cross the river but have failed, it's my hope that these pages will renew your desire and send you on your way again. Beginning over again brings no fault or criticism to the traveler.

We will succeed if we try only one more time than we fail. Starting again is often the only thing we need to do. The serpent in the river can be beaten, especially when we journey together.

The first chapter in this book explores how and why we were made, examining our original relationship with God, as a child made in His image. We will learn more about what this image means and how it will play a vital role in our eventual "re-awakening." This image, we will see, is the basis for our true self, and the starting point for living a life the way we were meant to live it. In Chapter 2 we continue to develop our understanding of what it means to be a complete human being as we explore our physical and spiritual components and our transition from soil to soul. We'll see in Chapter 3 how God completes the human and readies him for the task of life by making him aware of his masculine-feminine blend. Chapter 4 discusses how God created the opportunity for us to grow spiritually and exercise our moral choice. Now that the stage has been set and the key players are ready, Chapter 5 describes the first encounter with the serpent, the moment of truth we all face, when the serpent entices us to surrender to its wishes rather than the will of God. The ego is born. The consequences of this choice are revealed in Chapter 6 where we will discuss the world of the ego and what impact it has on our lives and the world in general. The key to reclaiming what we once had in Eden is discussed in Chapter 7 (with a surprise ending!). Chapter 8 provides a study of five spiritual postures, key techniques in the awakening process. We conclude this book in Chapter 9 by providing a summary of the garden of Eden story as well as some guidance in finding the next stone across the river. The re-awakening process has begun, and the ideas in the final chapter can be used to help you and others along the journey.

Writing a book of this nature needs to be done with some hesitation on my part, and reading it needs to be done with some graciousness on the reader's part. This isn't because what has been written is of little value, but rather because it asks us to stretch our awareness of what is possible and to look at old stories in a new way. This becomes more complicated by the fact that one discovery reveals a path to another, and then another, and yet another. (This follows the principle of all-things-are-connected in this world, which is part of the Image of God.) If we were to attempt to capture all the possible threads of thought on these subjects the original goal of the book may be lost on an unintended side road. Therefore, I am keeping to the main path in this work, using the garden of Eden as our main discussion point, noting along the way where we could possibly go on another day's adventures.

Although the story of the garden of Eden is one of the oldest known to mankind, it may also be one of the most important stories for us today. The human civilization is in great need of spiritual guidance, direction and understanding which the events in the Eden story may provide; a revelation in psychological and spiritual awareness which has to be the basis for our living together in peace and harmony. This book offers a new perspective to an old story, so, as you travel these pages, look for insights regarding the relationship between Adam and Eve, the role of the serpent, and the possibility that we have the power within us to reclaim Eden.

Daniel D. Schroeder

1. Imago Dei

When I look at your heavens,
The work of your fingers,
The moon and the stars that you have established;
What are human beings that you are mindful of
    them,
Mortals that you care for them?
Yet you have made them a little lower than the
    divine beings,
And crowned them with glory and honor.
You have given them dominion over the works
    of your hands;
You have put all things under their feet,
All sheep and oxen,
And also the beasts of the field,
The birds of the air, and the fish of the sea,
Whatever passes along the paths of the seas.

(Psalm 8:3-8)

"The image of God is found essentially and personally in all mankind. Each possesses it whole, entire and undivided, and all together not more than one alone. In this way we are all one, intimately united in our eternal image, which is the image of God and the source in us of all our life." Blessed John of Ruysbroeck

THE END WILL BE THE BEGINNING

The story of the garden of Eden isn't over. It will one day end where it began: all things will be brought back into the love of God, made perfect in His image, in complete unison and harmony. It can be no other way. God is love, and as such, "God will not take away a life; he will devise plans so as not to keep an outcast banished forever from his presence." (2 Samuel 14:14b) Imagine that! "He will devise plans so as not to keep an outcast banished forever from His presence." The implications of this verse dissolve the stronghold of the fear of eternal damnation of a wrathful, unforgiving God and replace it with the hope and compassion we can rightfully expect from a loving God. How He will accomplish this is beyond the scope of our intellect, but not beyond the understanding of our heart. Deep down inside, at the core of our being, we know this to be true.

> "For thus says the Lord God: I myself will search for my sheep, and will seek them out. As shepherds seek out their flocks when they are among their scattered sheep, so I will seek out my sheep. I will rescue them from all the places to which they have been scattered on a day of clouds and thick darkness." (Ezekiel 34:11-12)

What is this beginning in Eden which will also be the end? As it relates to us, His children, we will end up the way He intended us to be from the beginning: unique individuals that are spiritually connected to each other and to Him and to all of creation. Within each one of us is a specially designed soul that is built on a foundation of the gifts of the Holy Spirit: love, joy, peace, patience, kindness, generosity, faithfulness, gentleness and self-control. (Galatians 5:22) These gifts are the key attributes of the image of God, breathed into each one of us as we were being formed by Him. All His children share these same gifts. They were there at the beginning when we were made, they are there now (although sometimes covered up by an out-of-control ego), and they will be there when we pass from this life into the next. They are of God, and therefore indestructible. Along with these core gifts, He made each one of us in a very special and unique way with a personal set of interests and skills that could be used to serve Him in this life and the next according to a plan that He crafted. Our purpose in this life is to awaken to this truth, and then to live our lives according to these gifts. Our eternity, our road back to Eden, begins here and now.

GOD CREATES OUT OF LOVE

An old Islamic saying describes God's thoughts as He contemplated creating the universe: "I was a hidden treasure and I longed to be known, so I created the world." The fullness of love can not be contained. It has to create and expand so that it can be shared. God did not create us because He was lonely; He created us because it's the nature of love to find ways to express itself, and then to share in that love together. Love discovers all possible ways of expression. We see this clearly in the creation story as God sets out to express Himself through light, sky, earth, stars, creatures and plants. All things are of Him and from Him. The possibilities were endless, and the love flowed out in all directions through each new thing He created. And God saw how good it all was.

Perhaps He was putting the finishing touches on a herd of buffalo, or on His thousandth variety of flower when He said,

> "Let us make humankind in our image, according to our likeness; and let them have dominion over the fish of the sea, and over the birds of the air, and over the cattle, and over the wild animals of the earth, and over every

creeping thing that creeps upon the earth. So God created humankind in his image, in the image of God he created them; male and female he created them." (Genesis 1:26-27)

He must have spun around in delight at this thought, addressing the whole of His creation. It was another joyous idea in a string of millions. This human would be like the rest of creation because it would be made by the hands of God just as all the other things were made. The human would be connected to everything else because all things flowed out of the same Creator. Humankind would not be separate from nature, but would be a part of it.

"God blessed them, and God said to them, 'Be fruitful and multiply, and fill the earth and subdue it; and have dominion over the fish of the sea and over the birds of the air and over every living thing that moves upon the earth. See, I have given you every plant yielding seed that is upon the face of all the earth, and every tree with seed in its fruit; you shall have them for food. And to every beast of the earth, and to every bird of the air, and to everything that creeps on the earth, everything that has breath of life, I have given every green plant for food.' And it was so." (Genesis 1:28-30)

These humans would be not only expressions of God's love, but they themselves would be able to express

God's love to the rest of creation, through the creativity which God gave to them. They would care for the other things that God had made. They would gather food. They would learn about plants and animals, understanding how all lived together on the earth. They would see how all things formed an integrated system, and how all things were holy and to be respected, all having been created by God. Humans would have 'dominion' over other creatures because the humans would have a special connection and a shared understanding with God. This special connection would come to them through the gifts of love and creativity which God had given to them. That's what dominion meant – a special relationship, not unbridled power and authority.

God would not only have these new beings as part of His creation, but they could actually share in the love that was a part of Him. There would be a special connection between Him and these new beings. He found this idea to be very good and set about to bring it to reality.

THE IMAGE OF GOD

Humans would be created in God's image. But what is this image? How will this image reflect the nature of God?

"The imago Dei," writes Stephen Webb, professor of philosophy and religion at Wabash College, "assures us that there is an essential correlation between humanity and God that guarantees our basic intuitions into God's nature." [1]   Scanning a good portion of the material written on the image of God (and there is an abundance of it!), we can begin to shape our basic intuitions around three distinct aspects of this imago Dei. First, we're of the same essence as God. What He has given to us is a piece of Him. This is a holy thing, eternal and pure, and serves as our "power source," and they way we can come to know Him better. Second, because this image comes from Him, it's connected to Him. We are, in essence, His children. And because we're connected to Him, we're also connected to each other – to every other person who has received this image of God – and that is everyone. Therefore, we are all brothers and sisters, and He is Our Father. Third, because we are of Him and connected to Him, our purpose is the same as His. This image, this soul, is the gateway for the Holy Spirit to move through our lives and out into the world in service to Him. Our purpose together is to love as He has loved us. And although we all share in this identical image of God, He has also given to each of us very special and unique gifts. Our power as humans is limited, so if He divides the tasks among everyone, giving each person something special to do, then together His plan will get done. Our purpose is to first awaken to this fact, and then discover how we can serve Him in our own unique ways in our lives. To God, a smile or extending a helping hand for another person is just as important as building a hospital or saving a life. A gesture of thanks to another of His children is as important to Him as discovering the cure for a disease. "Truly I tell you, just as you did it to one of the least of these who are members of my family, you do it to me." (Matthew 25:40) Let us look a bit more closely now at each of these three aspects of the image of God: Essence, Connections, and Purpose.

ESSENCE

Essence consists of those attributes that are shared by both God and mankind. This was God's opportunity to expand some of His own essence to us in an act of loving grace. Since God is love, we can be certain that love is something He wanted us to have as well, and therefore love would be included in His image given to us. So, first of all, we're all capable of love. And what are the characteristics of love?

> "Love is patient; love is kind; love is not envious or boastful or arrogant or rude. It does not insist on its own way; it is not irritable or resentful; it does not rejoice in wrongdoing, but rejoices in the truth. It bears all things, believes all things, hopes all things, endures all things. Love never ends." (I Corinthians 13:4-8b)

These are the characteristics, the very essence, of each one of us. These are the fruits of the Holy Spirit. Love must be given freely or it isn't really love. Therefore, we would also have to have free will. Without free will, there can be no love because love has to be a choice. But this very same free will that enables us to move closer to God and others in love would also be the very same free will which could separate us from God if used wrongly.

"Lord, You have given me my being of such a nature that it can continually make itself more able to receive Your grace and goodness. And this power, which I have of You, wherein I have a living image of Your almighty power, is free will. By this I can either enlarge or restrict my capacity for Your grace." Nicholas of Cusa

This risk has a potentially high cost. But it's also a risk that *has* to be taken for the possibility of love to exist. To prepare humans for this responsibility, God had to equip us with a well-balanced set of tools and abilities that would provide us with a blend of physical, mental and spiritual perspectives. We would have the ability to reason and create. We would have free will. We would have love. But Before facing the actual test against the cunning serpent of temptation, God's human being would need something more. So part of the image of God given to mankind would include a complete masculine-feminine blend representing the physical-spiritual sides of the human.

"So God created humankind in his image, in the image of God he created them; male and female he created them." (Genesis 1:27)

Taken literally, this verse means that God created some humans as males, and some as females. That, of course, would allow them to fulfill God's request in verse 28 to "be fruitful and multiply." God could have designed the *physical* man to reproduce asexually for him to multiply and fill the earth, but He did not. Separate male and female forms are chosen instead. But it's also important to view verse 28 from a spiritual perspective. It says that God created man in His image. This was a divine image. There were not two gods, one male god and one female god. There was *one* God from whom humans were made. It could be reasoned that if one God made humans *in His image*, and this image contained both male and female attributes, then the complete image of God must contain both a masculine and a feminine side, and these were given to the human. (See also Genesis 5:1-2) From a *spiritual* perspective, it's important to understand that the complete separation into two spiritual genders according to physical gender isn't necessary, and perhaps ill-advised. Just as we have seen that God has a masculine and a feminine side in His image, so do we, to varying extents, contain both elements of masculinity and femininity as part of the image we inherited from God.

To fully understand the true nature of our selves, whether we're physically a male or a female, we gain a tremendous advantage by opening to the possibility that there are masculine and feminine aspects to our spiritual and mental design just as there are in God's. This will not detract from who we are. Recognizing these two sides in us will actually add to who we already are. This is the image of God! This is who we are as beings made in that image.

Robert Alter writes in *Genesis: Translation and Commentary*, "In the middle clause of this verse [Genesis 1:27], 'him' as in the Hebrew, is grammatically but not anatomically masculine. Feminist critics have raised the question as to whether here and in the second account of human origins in Genesis 2, 'Adam' is to be imagined as sexually undifferentiated until the fashioning of woman..."[2] Alter goes on to suggest that this proposal leads to some "dizzying paradoxes" in the ensuing story. And yet, when we view this from the proper spiritual perspective, we'll see that it can make all the sense in the world.

The interaction between our masculine and feminine sides in each one of us will play a critical role in taming the serpent in our lives. Taming this serpent is the key to awakening to our true selves, and to reclaiming the spiritual birthright in God's image that is our destiny. This will become clearer as we continue our journey back to the garden of Eden.

Substantively, then, we can argue that the image of God will include a spiritual essence made up of love and compassion, free will, reason, and a physical-spiritual blend.

CONNECTIONS

The connective characteristic of the imago Dei is the result of our shared essence with God. It represents a relationship that extends not only to every person on the planet, but to every creature and every thing as well. Because we all come from the One Creator we're all connected. He is Our Father, and we are His children.

It has been said that "blood is thicker than water," which suggests a stronger bond among blood relatives than among friends. And we sometimes see that "money is thicker than blood," as when the bonds of family dissolve over money issues – squabbling over inheritance, dividing windfalls, or even simple family budgeting matters.

The connective characteristic of the imago Dei is something that transcends both blood and money. In one sense it brings us all the way back to the unity that is achieved through the simplest of elements, water. This is the holy water that makes us all one family. There is no higher association than the association with God and His creation. Keeping our focus at that higher level when we deal with personal, national, or global issues changes our perspective *because* we are all *one* family, *one* body, with *one* Father. When we forget this, either as individuals or as a nation, we begin to crumble. Scripture and the newspapers are replete with examples of what happens when we turn our backs on God. The changes we could make in this world and in our own lives would be immense if each one of us individually always remembered our connectivity to everyone and everything else in our lives. It goes beyond just our own household, community state or nation. Imago Dei is meant to show our connectedness with God and each other. "The rich and poor have this in common: the Lord is maker of them all." (Proverbs 22:2)

Everything is connected with everything and with everyone else. What we do on a large scale to the rain forest, for example, impacts the global environment. Even what we do on an individual scale ultimately contributes to a larger scale impact on a collective basis. The garbage we throw away, the food we eat, even the thoughts we think affect the whole.

Not only is everything connected to everything else, but everything is also connected with the Creator. Everything came from this source, so everything is connected to it. "I am the vine, you are the branches. Those that abide in me and I in them bear much fruit, because apart from me you can do nothing." (John 15:5)

And if everything is connected to the Creator, then when we label things as "good" or "bad" in a moral sense, it can lead us to gross errors and injustices. Even though we will always be connected with God and all of His creation, sometimes in our minds we begin to believe that we're separate beings, unconnected to anyone or to anything and have the right and power to discern good from bad. When we partake in this separation, we forget that we're children of God, created in His image. When this happens, we open the door for "bin" type thinking; the kind of thinking that puts everything into separate categories, that allows for labels, prejudices, fears, biases, and crippling attachments;

the kind of thinking that puts ourselves into one bin (the "good" bin), and puts everything else outside of this bin. Perhaps this is why we're severely warned in the garden of Eden not to attempt to assume this knowledge: "But of the tree of the knowledge of good and evil you shall not eat, for in the day that you eat of it you shall die." (Genesis 2:17) Moral judgment needs to be left in the hands of the One who can most aptly discern it.

PURPOSE

The shared essence and connectivity with God begs to be put to use because this is the nature of love and creativity. As part of God's family, we become co-creators with Him. No, we cannot make stars or planets, or bring life to a rock. But as the human race, we have been given responsibilities over *some* aspects of nature. Recall that God gave us 'dominion' over the birds, and the cattle, and the fish. We are to care for, and replenish these gifts, giving thanks to God for all He has given to us, and being good stewards of all creation. Psalms and other scripture are full of God's declarations asserting His rule over all of nature.

Has the concept of the imago Dei been viewed as our license to rise *above* nature? Have we viewed this as the permission we need to separate ourselves from nature rather than living as part of it? Man apart from nature, rather than as part *of* nature, is a recipe for trouble. Our attempt to go beyond nature and put ourselves in a 'god-like' rule over nature usually ends in disaster. Consider the great dust bowl of the 1930's in the United States, or the drying of lakes, the depletion of aquifers, or climate change. The examples of our unwillingness to live with nature and the harm that this unwillingness does are abundant.

Our purpose as co-creators with God, as individuals who are part of the image of God, is to "love the Lord your God with all your heart, and with all your soul, and with all your mind...And you shall love your neighbor as yourself." (Deuteronomy 6:5 and Matthew 22:37-40) If humans love God, and if all humans are an expression of God (their true selves), then we're to love all humans. If nature is an expression of God, then we're to love and care for it, too. We fulfill our purpose by being who God created us to be, our true selves, and by serving Him in our own unique way. We find our way by eliminating cultural noise and years of programming, and begin to listen to our inner soul, the image of God built into us. More on this later.

> "I have maintained ere this and I still maintain that I already possess all that is granted to me in eternity. For God in the fullness of his Godhead dwells eternally in his image – the soul." Meister Eckhart

OUR UNIQUE IMAGE

Human beings are made in the image of God, but that does not make them God. Scripture does not say that all the characteristics and attributes of God's image will appear in us. That honor belongs to Christ alone (Hebrews 1:3). We can learn more about ourselves and the image of God when we learn more about Christ. But the totality of God is unknowable, so even though we learn more about ourselves and Christ, we do not learn it all.

We do know, however, that each one of us was created individually by God, and that He gave each of us a set of interests, talents and skills that He would like us to use to serve Him both in this life and in the next. When we live our lives according to the plan that He designed, we find the peace, joy, and fulfillment that are our spiritual birthright. To know who we truly are and to bring that to life is to glorify God. This is the special purpose that we all share. This is the path to reclaiming Eden. "God saw everything that he had made, and indeed, it was very good. And there was evening and there was morning, the sixth day." (Genesis 1:30)

2 From Soil to Soul

"Do you not know that you are God's temple
and that God's Spirit dwells in you?
(I Corinthians 3:16)

"My Me is God, nor do I recognize any other
Me except my God Himself."
St. Catherine of Genoa

The image of God now becomes the soul of mankind. A treasure of great value, this precious pearl from God would be placed within the clay man to turn him from soil to soul. The potter gives life to His clay jar:

"Then the Lord God formed man from the dust of the ground, and breathed into his nostrils the breath of life; and the man became a living being." (Genesis 2:7)

In an intimate act between the Lover and beloved, the Creator God moved close to the human and began a relationship with him that would last forever. It began with the gift of His perfect image to mankind, and would be sustained by the power of His Spirit. For each and every one of His children, God performs this very same act. As we were being "knitted in our mother's womb," (Psalm 139) God breathed into us the breath of life that contained not only the key components of His image discussed in the last chapter, but also a very unique set of skills, talents, interests and preferences. This is what makes us who we are. It changed us from dust into people – from soil into souls.

THE BREATH OF LIFE

The breath of life is used to place the image of God into the soul of the human, where the true self exists. The image of God that was put into the human contained all the gifts of the Holy Spirit. We know these to be love, joy, peace, patience, kindness, generosity, faithfulness, gentleness, and purity. (Galatians 5:22-23) This is our spiritual birthright and heritage. This is what has been given to us freely and is ours to enjoy eternally. This is the pure self, the part that is connected to God because it is *of* God. It's the part of us that is pure and chaste; the part where free will makes love possible. It's the natural state of every person – the perfect image of a perfect God, egoless and good. It's how we began our existence, and it's the state to which we will all return one day.

The essence of our soul is the same as the essence of God – love. This love is the part of the soul and the image of God that is common to all of us. We each share in this universal quality that is the driving force behind all creation. But it's also perhaps one of the things we struggle with the most. Just what exactly is "love?" What does it mean to me? How am I supposed to use it? Is what I am doing really pleasing to God? The great commandment to love God with all your heart and with all your soul and with all your mind, and to love our neighbor as yourselves, (Matthew 22:37-40) brings with it the basic question, "How?"

Love is more of a state of being than it is an action. Yes, it results in specific actions that are unique to a particular situation in a moment of time, but these actions stem from a place where we are fully connected to God. The closer we are to our true selves, to the very image of God, the more loving actions will automatically flow from us, regardless of where we are or when it is. To love God and to love your neighbor and to love yourself means that you are in a state of high connectivity with them, unencumbered by the desires, prejudices, judgments, biases, fears, or guilt of a dysfunctional ego. It means that you are experiencing the fruits of the Holy Spirit in your moment to moment life. When you are in this state of awareness and connectivity, the needs of the moment that you can do something about will be apparent to you, and the resources needed to do them will also be at hand. You are where you are supposed to be to contribute your piece to God's plan. You will know what needs to be done through love as the moment plays out. The prayer of St. Francis expresses this well:

> "Lord, make me a channel of thy peace;
> that where there is hatred, I may bring love;
> that where there is wrong, I may bring the spirit
>   of forgiveness;
> that where there is discord, I may bring harmony;
> that where there is error, I may bring truth;
> that where there is doubt, I may bring faith;
> that where there is despair, I may bring hope;
> that where there are shadows, I may bring light;
> that where there is sadness, I may bring joy.

Lord, grant that I may seek rather to comfort
    than to be comforted;
to understand, than to be understood;
to love, than to be loved.
For it is by forgetting self that one finds.
It is by forgiving that one is forgiven.
It is by dying that one awakens to eternal life.
                            Amen."

KEY CHARACTERISTICS

There are several characteristics of love that can be highlighted to gain a better understanding of it. First is the fact that loving actions are unique to the individual. The lamp gives light, not shade. But the tree gives shade. Flowers give fragrance and beauty. We each have been given special gifts – many different things to further God's creation – none of which is small or insignificant. Consider where St. Paul speaks about the variety of gifts, the varieties of services, and the varieties of activities we all do, even though it's the same God who "activates all of them in everyone." It's the Holy Spirit that allots to the individual just as She chooses, but we're all still one body with many members, working for the good of God.

"Indeed, the body does not consist of one member but of many. If the foot would say, 'Because I am not a hand, I do not belong to the body,' that would not make it any less a part of the body. And if the ear would say, 'Because I am not an eye, I do not belong to the body,' that would not make it any less a part of the body. If the whole body were an eye, where would the hearing be? If the whole body were hearing, where would the sense of smell be? But as it is, God arranged the members in the body, each one of them, as he chose. If all were a single member, where would the body be? As it is, there are many members, yet one body."

(I Corinthians 12:14-20)

If you love to make music, then it's your music that is an act of love. If you love to build things, then it's your building of them that is an act of love. If you love to be nice to people you meet on the street, it's your courtesy that is an act of love. Be who you are, and your love will flow.

Second, love is indifferent. The light of the lamp shines on anyone who happens to pass by, whether they are "good" or "bad" in our minds. The tree offers shade to any who sit under it. The music of the violin soothes the ears of anyone within its range. Love doesn't pick or chose who gets served. If we begin to make decisions about who is worthy of our love and who isn't, we once

again fall into the Eden trap of the "knowledge of good
and evil." Your love needs to flow during the moment
it's needed as the situation beckons. We do not know the
impact our loving acts may have on the recipients of
them; we do not know what plans God may have had at
that moment for the person receiving it. Do your loving
acts out of joy and let the spiritual energy take its course.

Third, love is free. The lamp gives its light and
asks for nothing in return. The tree offers its shade and
doesn't charge for it. The iris presents its beauty and
fragrance, demanding no toll. Acts of love come with
no expectation of something in return. We are not
saying that gainful employment is wrong, where a
service or work is performed in exchange for fair
compensation. What we're saying is that when you
perform an act of love, whether at work or not, it's done
without expecting a reciprocal return of value.
Hopefully, we receive a "thank you" response or some
other polite gesture if we do something nice for
someone, but whether they respond or not, the act of
love was given freely simply for the love of God. The
intention surrounding your act of love circulates very
positive spiritual energy that will generate further

occasions for loving actions elsewhere in place and time. If someone does reciprocate for a loving act that you performed, be sure to accept this graciously, and not refuse it, as this, too, keeps the positive energy flowing.

Fourth, love is continuous. The lamp shines whether there is someone in the room or not. The tree offers shade to a crowd or to the empty grass below. The iris is beautiful even if no one is looking at it. Love flows blissfully unaware of itself. It flows continuously because it's love. While we may have been taught to believe that this is waste, it is actually power. Love does not need a recipient, it just needs to flow. If you love to make music, then make music! If you need someone to hear you play, that may be your ego talking. If you love to fish, go fish! You do not need someone to see you fish. If you love to draw, then draw! If you give money to a worthy cause, try to do it anonymously. God knows you did it. Of course, if your love is to help people, then you may need them around to do it. But aren't there ways to help others when they are not around? So, if you're short of people for the moment, but there is a way that is before you to help someone else, go help! Love has no shut-off valve.

Finally, love is undemanding. The lamp will not drag someone into its light, nor will the tree pull someone under its branches for shade. The iris will not stuff itself up someone's nose. We may have an irresistible urge to force our love onto someone else because we know that what we have to offer is exactly what they need – or at least we think so. The recipient of forced love will not view it as such, nor will it have the desired effect on that person. This can be frustrating, especially when the need and solution appears obvious. But what we think is obvious is perhaps a product of misguided judgment. Allow the Holy Spirit to do Her work in placing people in the path of oncoming love at the right time and right place. Keep the first four characteristics in mind and step aside. The best way to convince others that a life following the will of God is the best way to go can not be achieved through argument or controversy. That may actually do more harm than good. The best way, and perhaps the only way to convince them, suggests Aldous Huxley, is to experience the fruits of the Holy Spirit in your own life: "Only those who manifest their possession, in however small a measure, of the fruits of the Spirit can persuade others that the life of the Spirit is worth living."[3]

SIN AND CONNECTEDNESS

St. Paul tells us in his letter to the Romans, "For I am convinced that neither death, nor life, nor angels, nor rulers, nor things present, nor things to come, nor powers, nor height, nor depth, nor anything else in all creation, will be able to separate us from the love of God in Christ Jesus our Lord." (Romans 8:38-39) The connection between God and mankind is unbreakable and permanent. This connection comes by means of the image of God in us, that piece of Himself that He shares with our souls. And as we read in I Corinthians 6:17, "But anyone united to the Lord becomes one spirit with him."

Our true self, the part of us that is the soul, comes from God, is the same essence as God, and is therefore perfect in Him. When we're in alignment with God, fully connected with Him, we're in a sinless state. The soul that is connected to God through the Holy Spirit can not sin. How could it? If it's fully connected with God, then it's always doing the will of God. If it becomes disconnected from God (by our choice), then it has the potential for not doing God's will, and this is more commonly known as "sinning." Sin starts out as a state of separation from God. The more that we are separated from God, the more we can be said to be in a state of sin. This can, and often does, lead to acts of sin, which is how we usually view sin. Rather than focusing on the act of sinning, however, it's much more beneficial to focus on the proximate cause of sinning in the first place, and that is our separation from God. Those whose behavior we often refer to as "sinful" are more likely than not in a state of disconnectedness from God.

The word "sin" itself carries an aura of judgment. If we hear that a person is a sinner there is an immediate negative connotation with that label. Part of us wants to withdraw from that person because we don't want to be associated with anyone deemed "bad." We may feel that it will infect us. Another part of us may fear that we, too, will be accused of the same fault, so we want to avoid any association with the guilty person. Or, we may feel the swelling of guilt or shame growing within us, knowing that we, too, at some point *may* have done something similar, or are *like* the guilty person, and we know that someone, somewhere will disapprove.

Thomas Merton writes that "sin is the refusal of spiritual life, the rejection of the inner order and peace that comes from our union with the divine will. It's the refusal of God's will and His love. It is more radically a refusal to be what we are, a rejection of our mysterious, contingent, spiritual reality hidden in the very mystery of God. It's our refusal to be what we were created to be – children of God, images of God."[4] The root of it all is that people are looking for themselves, in the content of their own lives, rather than God's. There is an inborn desire and craving to identify with something. God meant it to be Him, but we look for it instead in the content of our physical life. The truth is obscured by this desire.

Labeling someone's behavior as "sinful" is a weapon of manipulation and control. It serves to raise the egos of those people who can, for the present, use the label against others whose difficulties have come to light. It serves to place those falling within sin's grasp under the influence and control of institutions that have the authority to redeem. Labeling someone a sinner is often a sin in itself. Labeling someone a sinner causes us to think about the next step: punishment, containment and/or retribution. It's a natural sequence of our human thinking to move from pronouncing guilt to extracting recompense. The strength of our personal and family relationships are also often weighed by who did what to whom, and how they haven't made up for it yet. We'll get even, some day, by golly! Our entire society is built on this system of justice.

God's system of justice is based on different principles. His primary goal isn't to make sure that sinners are punished and the sinner beaten into submission; His main interest is that the "sinner" is reconnected with the power of their own soul, that the flow of the Holy Spirit is renewed, and that the person is once again living their true self. The reconnected person will make things right for those that she or he may have faulted. There will be no need to impose penalties or a pound of flesh; in a fully connected system, all debts will be settled properly in a fair and just manner. In man's system the sinner is viewed as being bad and needing to be punished; in God's system the sinner is viewed as being lost and needing to be reconnected.

Mankind interprets Romans 6:23 (For the wages of sin is death…) as being the physical and eternal death that a person deserves for being a sinner. God, on the other hand, is trying to emphasize that if you are sinning (that is, in a state of separation from Him), you are not living your true life, but a false one. Your true life is dead. Sin and connectedness are inversely related. There is a greater potential for sin the less we're connected with God. The goal for God is to return us all to a state of connectedness. The more we're connected with God, the more we will be living our true life.

SIX BILLION TEMPLES

In I Samuel 3, young Samuel, a novice in the service of the Temple, was awakened several times during the night by the gentle voice of God calling his name. He was given a message for Eli, a priest in the Temple. The message was not good news for Eli, (he was going to lose his power as a priest for failing to guide his sons) but the context with which the message was received by Samuel is good news for us. First, we see that God is persistent in His attempt to reach us. He doesn't quit very easily. As long as there is a chance that we will listen, He will speak. Second, the Almighty God who created the entire cosmos is also intimately attached to us, calling us by name to attract our attention and establish a relationship. Samuel! Samuel! Third, God speaks to us in the Temple. In the Hebrew scriptures this was the one and only Temple in Jerusalem. As our understanding of God evolves, however, we're taught in the New Testament that WE are actually the temple of God. Remember: "Do you not know that you are God's temple and that God's Spirit dwells in you?" (I Corinthians 3:16) It's actually within us, within our soul, where God speaks. It's through the soul that He placed in us with the breath of life that He speaks to us. The kingdom of God is within you. To hear Him, we need to be still and know that He is God. (Ps. 46:10)

If each of us is a temple of God, then there isn't one temple, but over six billion of them on this earth. Talk about a spiritual Internet! Think of the power and good that could be done if we were all fully connected with God, each person accepting God's principles of love; each person manifesting the fruits of the Holy Spirit. This collective temple would make us all truly one family under God moving us ever closer to a restored Eden. But we have a long way to go to reach this point. It begins, of course, on the individual level with you and me. It begins by understanding what it means to be a temple of God.

Thomas Merton pointed out that if we are to become reconnected with God, to become truly humble, we must become fully who we really are – the person God made us to be – so that we can fully serve Him in a way that He needs us to serve Him. Finding our true selves will bring us humility, and learning to be humble will help us to find ourselves. That is why we try to work at both. Contrary to what we are occasionally told by motivational speakers, teachers or other leaders, we *cannot* be anything we want to be in life. The truth is that we must be what we were meant to be, what God made us to be. There is no other way to peace. "However that may be, let each of you lead the life that the Lord has assigned, to which God called you." (I Corinthians 7:17) Being a temple of God means coming back to what our purposes in life are; first, to awaken to the fact that we are a temple of God (one of six billion on the earth), and second, to serve God in joy by using our own special, unique abilities, talents, interests and preferences in a loving way to further His creation as His willing servant. This is how we glorify God.

SOIL TO SOUL TO SERVANT

We change from soil to soul when God breathes into us His image. We change from soul to servant when we awaken to His love, and begin to live the life He gave to us – a life that is unique and special – a life that will add to His Kingdom. The Kingdom of God is within us, says Jesus, because we are the temple of God. The Kingdom of God is expanded to those around us, because we live who we really are. When we're fully connected to God, a channel is opened through our soul whereby the grace and love of the Holy Spirit can flow out into the world. As She flows through each one of us, Her acts of love and creation take on special and unique characteristics that reflect who we truly are. The variety and diversity that results is truly amazing.

Christ's emptying himself out in love for all of us is a classic example of this life. The Greek word *kenosis* refers to the idea of a person ridding themselves of anything that isn't of God – of emptying themselves out so that the uninterrupted love of God can flow through them into the world. As it does so, it's shaped and colored by the individual skills, talents and interests that were given to us. So, for each person, the result may be different, but it's still part of the overall loving plan of God.

One piece yet remains to be given to mankind as God prepares humans to face the world, and this is a more complete understanding of who they are. We will see how this takes place in the garden of Eden as we explore the next chapter.

3 One Plus One Equals One

"Spirits without bodies will never be spiritual men and women. It is our entire being, that is to say, the soul and the flesh combined, which by receiving the Spirit of God constitutes the spiritual person."

Irenaeus of Lyons, *Against Heresies*, V, 8, 2

"The Valley Spirit never dies.
It is called the Mysterious Female.
And the doorway of the Mysterious Female
is the base from which Heaven and Earth spring.
It is there within us all the time.
Draw upon it as you will; it never runs dry."

Lao Tzu

THE GIFT OF AWARENESS

When we look at the story of Adam and Eve metaphorically, we see that it's really a story about each one of us individually. Viewed in this challenging way, each person has an Adam side (the physical nature) and an Eve side (the spiritual nature). We see that each human was given a body made from the dust of the earth (the Adam side) so that he or she could be a part of the physical world, moving and existing among the plants and animals. This body could be a male or female with variations in shape size and structure, but it's still a physical thing. Contained within this body is the marvelous human mind, a neural network that can collect, analyze, and store information in countless ways. This mind coordinates movement and balance, senses fear and danger, and regulates body systems needed to keep the body alive. The human was also given a soul made from the breath of God, containing the image of God, so that the person could love and stay connected with God. This soul was the channel through which God's energy could flow, and the work of the Holy Spirit could be accomplished in a unique and special way through each person, whether their physical body was male or female. The two separate parts of the human can be compared:

Physical Nature	Spiritual Nature
• Has a body consisting of arms, legs, head, torso, etc., could be male or female	• Consists of the soul containing the image of God

- Has a brain used as a thinking tool for capturing, storing, and analyzing information
- Source of urges, instincts and drives related to safety, food, reproduction, etc.
- Often referred to as the "head side"
- The body is a "form" and will therefore one day change like all forms; it will return to the earth

- It is the place where free will choice is made

- Also contains desires of a higher order, such as justice, equality, and peace
- Often referred to as the "heart side"
- The soul is essence and is therefore eternal; it will one day return to God

There remained only one thing more the human needed, and this was to join these two sides, the physical and spiritual, into a unified whole. These two pieces had to work together in harmony for the human to be fully functional. This joining would be accomplished through the gift of awareness.

The gift of awareness is what makes us truly human. First, it's our ability to recognize that we're not just physical creatures or just spiritual creatures. We are both. We are an integrated whole, a joining of different parts. We are a combination of flesh and spirit. A truly healthy life is one that nurtures and uses both sides.

Second, awareness also reminds us that even though we're an integrated whole, each part of us still has a specific function to perform, and they should not get mixed up. This is particularly true when we consider the relationship between the brain and soul. These two should work together, but they also need to stay distinct. Awareness gives us the ability to separate our true self (our soul) from our mental reactions (our mind) as we interact with people and situations; awareness gives us the ability to separate our true self from our physical urges, desires, and instincts. Awareness is *the* critical factor for us to live in harmony with nature and with others, and it will be *the* critical factor for us to eventually awaken from the runaway ego of our mind and to reconnect with God through our soul. We need the power of awareness to distinguish between our ego's thoughts and our own. Without the gift of awareness we may miss our opportunity to reconnect with God; without awareness we become "spiritually asleep" even though we move and talk and eat. It is awareness that brings us true light. Therefore, the gift of awareness is the beginning step to our personal salvation.

RECEIVING THE GIFT

The last half of Genesis 2 describes how Eve, the woman, was made from Adam's rib:

"Then the Lord God said, 'It is not good that the man should be alone; I will make him a helper as his partner.' So out of the ground the Lord God formed every animal of the field and every bird of the air, and brought them to the man to see what he would call them; and whatever the man called every living creature, that was its name. The man gave names to all cattle, and to the birds of the air, and to every animal of the field; but for the man there was not found a helper as his partner. So the Lord God caused a deep sleep to fall upon the man, and he slept; then he took one of his ribs (sides) and closed up its place with flesh. And the rib (side) that the Lord God had taken from the man he made into a woman and brought her to the man. Then the man said, 'This at last is bone of my bones and flesh of my flesh; this one shall be called Woman, for out of Man this one was taken.'" (Genesis 2:18-23)

Literal interpretations of scripture, especially when they are filled with imagery such as this part of the Eden story, fail to grasp the full richness of its meaning. The literal interpretations of this story have been used to claim that men are superior to women. The belief is that the woman was created after the man, and she was made from a rib of the man as though she was an afterthought, and that the breath of life was breathed into the man, and not the woman. This interpretation creates unnecessary divisions, causing us to overlook entirely what God is trying to teach us about ourselves. God's love unites – not divides.

So, what is this segment of the Eden story *really* telling us? When viewed spiritually, this part of the garden of Eden story is actually describing how God gave people the gift of awareness. It's the story of how God first made the human aware of both the body and soul, and how they were parts of each one of us. This is the story of how God instilled an appreciation of this unity into the person so that no aspect (body or soul) would ignore or dominate the other. A life of balance is achieved when the body and soul are functioning as one. God intends for us to live in both the physical and spiritual realms while we walk the earth because they are both needed to make us fully human. As Irenaeus of Lyons suggested in the opening quote to this chapter, it takes both a body and a soul to make a complete person.

A NEW PARTNERSHIP

Let's look at this part of the Eden story again, keeping in mind the spiritual perspective (sometimes referred to as a "unitive" perspective where all things are related in some sense). The literal perspective (sometimes referred to as a 'binary' perspective) is where things are either this or that, one or the other and not really related. Although the literal perspective has a place in acquiring knowledge, it often falls short in furthering understanding. So, rather than viewing this as a story about two separate individuals, Adam and Eve, let's consider that this is a story about two sides of *one* individual – the physical part consisting of body-mind combination, and the spiritual part consisting of a soul. Both the physical side and the spiritual side have unique qualities that are needed to complete us as humans since we have been created in God's image. When we say this, we are referring back to the image of God described in Genesis:

> "So God created humankind in his image, in the image of God he created them; male and female he created them." (Genesis 1:27)

Many scholars and writers down through the years considered the spiritual side of our selves as feminine, and the physical side as masculine. Aldous Huxley explains this universal idea about a feminine soul in *The Perennial Philosophy:* "In every exposition of the Perennial Philosophy [common threads in religious thought carried down through the ages in the world's major religions] the human soul is regarded as feminine in relation to the Godhead, the personal God and even the Order of Nature."[5]

In Genesis 2:18 we read, "Then the Lord God said, 'It is not good that the man should be alone; I will make him a helper as his partner ["help meet" in some translations].'" Robert Alter explains that the Hebrew *'ezer kenegdo* ("help meet") is notoriously difficult to translate.[6] In trying to understand the ancient Hebrew text we find room for the possibility that the human, made from mud, needed something more. The human's 'help meet' would be its guiding soul, a direct line to God.

From a spiritual perspective, we are taken back to the point in creation where God formed the human from the dust of the earth, making all his physical parts. But God wanted this human to have something very special in him, something He knew the human would need to remain connected with God and to help spread God's love and creativity. The human would need a special partner, a link between God's Kingdom and the physical realm. This link would be the human soul. The human needed to grow into the understanding that to make him a complete living being he had to fully integrate his physical part with his spiritual side.

To complete this understanding the human would need the gift of awareness, which the human had to be taught. Sometimes to help a student know what something is, a teacher will show the student what it's not. These contrasts help define boundaries and clarify description. This helps to build a baseline of understanding before the teacher moves ahead by narrowing the field of what is to be discussed. It gives the learner something with which to compare and to contrast. God used this "reverse" method of teaching to create awareness in Adam by first showing him where he *wouldn't* find a partner:

> "So out of the ground the Lord God formed every animal of the field and every bird of the air, and brought them to the man to see what he would call them; and whatever the man called

every living creature, that was its name. The man gave names to all cattle, and to the birds of the air, and to every animal of the field; but for the man there was not found a helper as his partner." (Genesis 2:19-20)

God wanted the human to fully understand that a true partnership would not come from some thing or some one outside of him. The partnership would be made with what was already inside of the human. To show him this, God made and brought to the human all the other creatures of the planet, showing each one to him. In doing so, the human was made aware that even though these other creatures were made by God, they could not provide him with the type of partnership the human needed. The human could now ask God, "If my helper and partner is not among these animals, then where is it?" Man's partner had to be something at a deeper level, more personal and closer to the heart. It had to be a soul, an image of God, which serves as the gateway to God. So, now it was time to bring this awakening to the man.

"So the Lord God caused a deep sleep to fall upon the man, and he slept; then he took one of his ribs [sides] and closed up its place with flesh. And the rib [side] that the Lord God had taken from the man he made into a woman and brought her to the man. Then the man said, 'This at last is bone of my bones and flesh of my flesh; this one shall be called Woman, for out of Man this one was taken.'" (Genesis 2:21-23)

In this teachable moment, God would have the human's full attention. To quiet the human's mind, God put him in a deep, contemplative state, one in which the human could look fully inward, down into the soul, to experience this coming revelation. The best translation of the Hebrew word *tzela* in these verses is "side" and not "rib". To find and fashion an appropriate partner for the man, God had to reach deep into the human near his heart to get the right material – more than just a rib – it was a whole side. God held the soul of the human in one of His hands and the body in the other, and brought them together as if to say, "Look! Look at your soul and your body. These are all gifts for you. These are meant to work together as one. You are a new creation of My doing. Therefore exist together in harmony and do My Will, and you shall enjoy the fruits of life!" The moral decision center of the human, the feminine-soul side, is united with the physical side through the gift of awareness and understanding.

It was at this point that the human actually became fully aware of its major components – the physical and spiritual which united the body and soul. This masculine-feminine relationship began in a spirit of companionship, not competition or sexuality. There was harmony, and there was health. This dual nature allows us to live in both the physical and spiritual realms – a unique place among God's creations. To fully understand this we have to be fully aware of it.

> "Therefore a man leaves his father and his mother and clings to his wife, and they become one flesh." (Genesis 2:24)

Metaphorically, this verse stresses the need for the body and the soul to unite as one person. The body and soul must exist together as one being, one person. The physical human unites with its own soul, becoming fully aware of itself. This full awareness hides nothing. There are no false parts, no cover-ups, no façades. The human is clothed with spiritual material, and isn't ashamed of what it sees: "And the man and his wife were both naked, and were not ashamed." (Genesis 2:25)

Through the gift of awareness, the body and soul of the person can now work together to fulfill their purpose. They will learn to function as one; they will make mistakes, but will learn from them. The moral decision-making capacity of the soul will learn to use the logic capabilities of the physical mind, the link between the soul and the body. Aldous Huxley reminds us, "There is a general agreement, East and West, that life in a body provides uniquely good opportunities for achieving salvation or deliverance."[7]

We will soon see how the brain, part of the physical side, gives rise to the thinking mind, a separate thought form, having a tendency to produce a continuous stream of ideas that offers many tempting possibilities for the soul unless it's harnessed properly. As the mind develops and improves its capabilities, it will even suggest that it take over and "run the show." The stage has now been set for the first adverse encounter between the mind and the soul, which will take place in the garden of Eden.

4 The Garden

"There is a river whose streams make glad the
    city of God,
the holy habitation of the Most High.
God is in the midst of the city;
it shall not be moved;
God will help it when the morning dawns."

(Psalm 46:4-5)

Jesus said to her, "Everyone who drinks this
water will be thirsty again, but those who drink
of the water that I will give them will never be
thirsty. The water that I will give will become in
them a spring of water gushing up to eternal
life." (John 4:13-14)

Reclaiming the gift of Eden is the path to
enlightenment. Finding our way back to Eden is the focus
of this book and perhaps the only worthwhile goal of our
lives. Why is Eden so important to us, and why did the
possibility exist from the beginning that we could lose it
through our own choice? Without understanding the

conditions for this perfect utopian gift, mankind is condemned to spend his entire life looking for, and struggling for, what was originally given to him freely by a loving God. History records the many failed attempts by man to achieve peace and security after rejecting God's plan. The trail through the millennia is littered with thousands of stories of pain and suffering, and they continue even today, marked by economic inequality, greed, famine and disease. These repeated failures on national and world levels are merely the collective result of individuals all looking for salvation in the wrong places.

THE BLESSINGS OF EDEN

The garden of Eden depicts the inevitable result of the fullness of God's presence and love in the physical world. In this ultimate blend of the spiritual realm with the physical realm we see an abundance of life, fertility, relationships, beauty, and peace. In Hebrew the name *gan-eden* means "garden of luxury, delight, fertility, and food dainties." When the fullness of God reigns on this earth there can be nothing but abundance and harmony. Here is how it's described in Genesis:

"And the Lord God planted a garden in Eden, in the east; and there he put the man whom he had formed. Out of the ground the Lord God made to grow every tree that is pleasant to the sight and good for food, the tree of life also in the midst of the garden, and the tree of the knowledge of good and evil." (Genesis 2:8-9)

First let's look at the blessings God wanted in the garden for His children, then we'll pay a visit to those two special trees mentioned in the later part of the passage. The garden of Eden would offer an abundance of food:

"Then God said, 'Let the earth put forth vegetation: plants yielding seed, and fruit trees of every kind on earth that bear fruit with the seed in it.' And it was so. The earth brought forth vegetation: plants yielding seed of every kind, and trees of every kind bearing fruit with the seed in it. And God saw that it was good." (Genesis 1:11-12)

There would also be an abundance of creatures:

"And God said, 'Let the waters bring forth swarms of living creatures, and let birds fly above the earth across the dome of the sky.' So God created the great sea monsters and every living creature that moves, of every kind, with which the waters swarm, and every winged bird of every kind. And God saw that it was good. God blessed them, saying, 'Be fruitful and multiply and fill the waters in the seas, and let birds multiply on the earth.' And there was evening and there was morning, the fifth day. And God said, 'Let the earth bring forth living creatures of every kind: cattle and creeping things and wild animals of the earth of every kind.' And it was so. God made the wild animals of the earth of every kind, and the cattle of every kind, and everything that creeps upon he ground of every kind. And God saw that it was good." (Genesis 1:20-25)

God wanted His garden to increase and multiply.

Not just the plants and animals, but mankind as well:

"God blessed them, and God said to them, 'Be fruitful and multiply, and fill the earth and subdue it; and have dominion over the fish of the sea and over the birds of the air and over every living thing that moves upon the earth.' God said, 'See, I have given you every plant yielding seed that is upon the face of all the earth, and every tree with seed in its fruit; you shall have them for food.'" (Genesis 1:28-31)

THE FOUR RIVERS

One of the other key features of Eden was the four rivers, or streams that flowed into the garden to water it.

"A river flows out of Eden to water the garden, and from there it divides and becomes four branches." (Genesis 2:10)

Although this may seem a trivial point, the direction of the river implied by the verse leads us to a key understanding about Eden. Ephraim Speiser writes in *The Anchor Bible*, "All four streams [branches] once converged, or were believed to have done so, near the head of the Persian Gulf, to create a rich garden land to which local religion and literature alike looked back as the land of the blessed."[8] Dr. Speiser earlier argued that the text in Genesis actually points to the fact that the four branches converged as they flowed *into* Eden, and that the text does not mean to imply that it was four branches coming *out* of Eden. Since this argument best fits the geographic facts of the presumed location of Eden, we can comfortably accept it and move on to the next question, which is, why these rivers or branches were mentioned in the first place.

> "The name of the first is Pishon; it is the one that flows around the whole land of Havilah, where there is gold; and the gold of that land is good; bdellium and onyx stone are there. The name of the second river is Gihon; it is the one that flows around the whole land of Cush. The name of the third river is Tigris, which flows east of Assyria. And the fourth river is the Euphrates." (Genesis 2:11-14)

Wouldn't it have been enough just to say that there was *a* river flowing into the garden? Why was it necessary to identify these four rivers? Was it to add credibility to the story making it more believable, or were the rivers symbolic of something else? The story of Eden would have worked just fine without having to specifically identify four rivers. Perhaps there is a level of meaning to explore here beyond the literal text that we see. Each of the rivers that converged on the garden formed the one river that 'watered' the garden, so each of them was contributing something vital to sustain the garden. Without further clues in the text, we are left with speculation.

Could it be that the four rivers feeding the garden of Eden represent God's openness and willingness to accept, and even encourage, the different human temperaments He knew His earthly children would have? Classifying human temperaments into groups isn't new. It may have started with the ancient Egyptians who connected personality differences to the four known elements at the time: earth, fire, water and air. Gradually personality types were associated with various bodily humours: blood, yellow bile, black bile and phlegm. These evolved into the four temperament types of sanguine, choleric, melancholic and phlegmatic, and were the basis of medicine for many centuries. Hippocrates was thought to have used them in the 4th century B.C. These ideas persisted largely through the writings of Galen, 131-201/217 AD. Down through the years there have been many theories regarding divisions of personality; Immanuel Kant, Rudolf Steiner, Alfred Adler, Erich Fromm, and Hans Eysenck to name a few. Most recently we see personality inventory tools such as the Keirsey Temperament Sorter and the Myers-Briggs Type Indicator (MBTI).

Perhaps the four rivers demonstrate that all types of people can be welcomed and nourished in the garden of Eden. The idea that these rivers flowed from different lands, each with special and unique characteristics, all joining together into one place to be in the presence of God, is very consistent with the overall inclusiveness of God. Implied in all this is a special invitation to all people to view their differences as a product of God's creativity; to welcome each other, to learn from each other, and to celebrate diversity.

The four rivers joining into the one that flows into the garden is a model for us to follow as individuals and as nations. To do anything less is to disconnect from God and His love by our own choice, cutting off the flow of those life-giving waters.

THE TWO TREES

"The Lord God took the man and put him in the garden of Eden to till it and keep it. And the Lord God commanded the man, 'You may freely eat of every tree in the garden; but of the tree of the knowledge of good and evil you shall not to eat, for in the day that you eat of it you shall die.'" (Genesis 2:15-17)

Now let's take a closer look at those two trees that were planted in the middle of the garden. Why did God give man this strange commandment not to eat of the tree of knowledge? Albertus Pieters writes, "The giving of this commandment was a part of God's perfect work in making man truly in His own image... In laying upon man this commandment God gave him an opportunity to do good, that is, to exercise his noblest capacity, as a free moral being."[9] Pieters goes on to explain that God gave man eyes, but if he had not made light, of what use would his eyes have been? The same argument could be used for the other senses as well. "How much the more, then, was it a good and gracious gift to furnish man with an opportunity for moral action!"[10]

Pieters's position is that man's conscience and free will would have had no opportunity to be used, tested, or grow if there had been no moral law given to him. Divine law was needed for mankind's free will to grow and strengthen just as light is needed for the eyes. Forbidding mankind to eat of the tree of knowledge of good and evil furnished him a precious opportunity to make right choices.

With the option to choose, however, there was also a danger of doing wrong. But this was a necessary risk to take, for without this possibility to exercise free will, there could be no love, for love only comes freely from the heart. Free will is a key ingredient in love. Gregory Boyd writes,

> "We have seen that the life God created humans to enjoy is centered on a provision and a prohibition. At the center of the garden were a tree of life and a forbidden tree. Our lives are meant to be centered on the confidence that God will share his eternal life with us as well as on the reverent acknowledgement that we are not to seek that which God reserves for himself. We are not to try to be God. We are to leave to God the knowledge of good and evil. The

fundamental cause and evidence of our separation from God, and thus the fundamental cause and evidence of our inability to receive and give the fullness of God's love, is that we violate this prohibition. We transgress the boundary God set between God and humanity."[11]

He goes on to explain that God's first concern, and really His only concern, is to have people who are united with Him in love. We are supposed to be participants with him in His love. The value of our lives comes from living out of love, not just living to be ethical.[12]

What does this all really mean? For me, the two trees in the garden represent the two ways of living from which we may freely choose. The garden is a gift to us, the way life is supposed to be. It is a blueprint for the entire earth. It is the ultimate and perfect gift from God the Creator to His creation; the perfect combination of the physical world with the spiritual world. All the needs of his children are met in this place: food, community, shelter, learning, safety – and most of all, it's a place where we can remain connected with God. It's a place where we can exercise our God-given senses, including our free will. This is the stage upon which we're placed to live and grow – and to challenge our power of choice. To sustain our presence in it, we simply eat from the Tree of Life. This is staying connected with God, wanting to live His way of living. Of this tree we may all freely eat. The gifts of the garden are not part of a "deal." They are not rewards for being good. They are simply the consequences of living a life the way it was meant to be lived. It's the natural order of things as designed from the beginning by a loving and compassionate God.

The other tree, the tree of knowledge of good and evil, represents our choice to go our own way, to live a life independent from God and independent from each other. This is mankind's "fall." It's our personal "fall." It's to allow ourselves a false sense of freedom based on an illusion created by a runaway ego. When we choose this path, things ultimately go wrong. These are not punishments, but natural consequences of being separated from our power source, Our Father. Certainly some who choose this path appear to prosper in the material world, at least for a time. But it's a life misplaced; a life that has been hollowed out and filled with weighty emptiness. Eventually it comes apart, leaving a disconnected, bereft soul.

5 The Birth of the Dysfunctional Ego

But he turned and said to Peter, "Get behind me, Satan! You are a stumbling block to me; for you are setting your mind not on divine things but on human things." Matthew 16:23

"Now the human soul cannot be alienated from God except through a mind enslaved by passions." Gregory of Nyssa, *The Lord's Prayer*

"Man's obsessive consciousness of, and insistence on being, a separate self is the final and most formidable obstacle to the unitive knowledge of God." Aldous Huxley, *Perennial Philosophy*

"The inner, basic, metaphysical defilement of fallen man is his profound illusory conviction that he is a god and that the universe is centered upon him." Thomas Merton, *The Silent Life*

INTRODUCING THE MIND

Up to this point we have seen how we are made up of both a physical side and a spiritual side. This combination of body and soul brings with it a special set of influences on our thoughts and behaviors. The challenge for each person lies in the fact that both body and soul have different interests and goals, and they're sometimes in conflict with one another. The body, for example, being a part of the physical world, shapes its needs and goals around things related to its preservation, satisfaction and reproduction. When God formed our bodies from the soil of the earth, He placed instincts, urges, and drives in us so that we could survive in the physical world. Without a feeling of hunger, for example, we may not eat and we would eventually perish. Without our sexual drives we would not procreate and our species would eventually vanish from the face of the earth. John speaks of this as the "will of the flesh." (John 1:13) In more recent times we know these to be natural instincts, urges and drives.

The soul, on the other hand, has its own needs. Being formed in the image of God, it seeks connections and equity. It looks for harmony among people and nature. It wants to create things and experiences in unique ways that further express the unity and love of God. It seeks beauty and peace. It strives to ensure that other people have the space and nurturing they need to become who they were meant to be. The soul part of us is designed to provide guidance and regulation to the body. It's attuned to social interaction and group needs. It has a sense of values and understands the interconnection of all things; it knows how we're connected to each other, how we're connected to the world and nature, and how we're connected to God our creator. The soul knows that in reality we are all one. While physical bodies seek others for self-preservation, souls seek others for community. So, although both the physical side and the spiritual side are created by God, the differences between them are significant enough that something else is needed to mediate the gap.

This is where the human brain plays a role by becoming the bridge between the physical and the spiritual. Thought processes of the brain are often referred to collectively as the mind. We view the mind as housing our personality, sometimes calling it our psyche or spirit. The mind is a wonderful gift that has far greater potential than we realize, but it also presents us with a set of dangers.

The mind receives information from the outside world through the five senses, and monitors the demands of the body as it senses hunger, pain, movement, fatigue, etc. When the mind is healthy, it dutifully collects and arranges information for us in a completely objective and reliable manner. It knows where to put each bit of information, and it retrieves it as it's needed. Thus, the mind serves as the liaison between us and the outside world, offering us this information in a steady stream of thought.

The mind is actually a rather marvelous gift. It's an amazing tool. It has a great responsibility to accurately detect and transmit information to us, and to carry out orders and instructions we give it. It's a highly intricate system that works in the present moment, but stores our experiences and information from the past, forming ideas and predictions about the future. Whether these past experiences were good or bad, the mind carefully stores them to be used to evaluate future dangers or potential opportunities.

THE SLIPPERY SLOPE

As we go through life, our mind continues to store vast amounts of information from the years and years of experiences. It's rather amazing how much detail is accumulated. As the mind organizes and processes this information, it provides a continuous stream of thoughts and memories for us to view. Because of this vast amount of information and experiences collected by the mind, it becomes expedient to begin to form associations, inferences, summaries and conclusions about what it knows. Information will sometimes be batched and woven together so that it can still fit into the stream of conscious thought. The mind is only trying to help us cope in a fast-paced world. (At least that's what the mind would like you to think.) The mind begins to add the role of commentator to that of information supplier.

Initially, many of these thought patterns may be quite good since they fit the facts at hand. They are logical conclusions based on years of experience. But these new thought patterns, blending into our consciousness, may or may not represent reality. We need to remember that the mind isn't concerned with reality; it's only concerned with information, which may or may not be true. It's designed to be an efficient handler of this information, to move it quickly through the system, and to summarize it for us to act on, for our own safety, needs and survival. It's our role to weigh the thoughts against reality and values – things we understand when we're fully connected with God. It's when we lose these connections that our sense of right and wrong becomes unclear. Having no other standard by which to live, we begin to accept the things we're thinking as the truth. Consciously, we begin to "fall asleep" on certain issues, allowing the mind to "call the shots."

It's at this point that a new player emerges within us – a serpent ego is born. It emerges from the mind to become a separate entity. The term "ego" may be used in different ways by different groups; it's commonly used today to describe a dysfunctional sense of self and that's how we'll use it in this book. It may have a tendency to overinflate our sense of self worth or undermine our self-esteem unnecessarily. The ego begins to build an existence of its own based on past experiences, and projects them into the future to meet its own needs. The ego becomes the new gatekeeper between the physical realm and the spiritual realm. It does not belong to either, and yet it's a part of both. Gradually we fall further into a state of isolation, thinking incorrectly that we're getting good information. The flow of truth diminishes, and slowly we become encased by an ever-expanding, dysfunctional ego with its collection of growing fears, desires, attachments, biases, guilt, shame and judgments.

THE REAL ORIGINAL SIN

Religious tradition records the encounter between the serpent ego and Eve in the garden of Eden as the "fall of man." The famous exchange taking place in the garden leads to what is commonly referred to as original sin. The serpent has sometimes been identified as the fallen angel, Lucifer, who now seeks to disrupt God's creation. Let's review the discussion between Eve and the serpent:

"Now the serpent was more crafty than any other wild animal that the Lord God had made. He said to the woman, 'Did God say, "You shall not eat from any tree in the garden?"' The woman said to the serpent, 'We may eat of the fruit of the trees in the garden; but God said, "You shall not eat of the fruit of the tree that is in the middle of the garden, nor shall you touch it, or you shall die."' But the serpent said to the woman, 'You will not die; for God knows that when you eat of it your eyes will be opened, and you will be like God, knowing good and evil.' So when the woman saw that the tree was good for food, and that it was a delight to the eyes, and that the tree was to be desired to make one wise, she took of its fruit and ate; and she also gave some to her husband, who was with her, and he ate. Then the eyes of both were opened, and they knew that they were naked; and they sewed fig leaves together and made loincloths for themselves." (Genesis 3:1-7)

Biblical scholar Robert Alter wrote that, "Eve enlarges the divine prohibition in another direction, adding a ban on *touching* to the one on eating, and so perhaps setting herself up for transgression: having touched the fruit, and seeing no ill effect, she may proceed to eat."[13] Remember that God didn't say Adam and Eve could not *touch* the fruit, they were just not supposed to eat it. The ego is already at work, already beginning to rationalize, in subtle steps, why the prohibition against eating from the tree isn't valid. Information reaching Eve is being tainted.

The serpent argues that God really knows that when the fruit of this tree is eaten, the eater's eyes will be opened, and the eater will then be more like God, "knowing good and evil." The irony of this lie, like many lies, is that being in a state of grace with God they are *already like God*. By falling prey to the promptings of the serpent, the end result is exactly the opposite of the promised benefit. In fact, once eating the fruit they become separated from God by having chosen a claim to the knowledge of good and evil. The serpent created a judgment about God. He planted a seed of doubt about God. The serpent implied that that is how God got His knowledge. The prohibition, argued the serpent, was merely to protect God's own status.

The serpent has convinced Eve to eat the fruit of the tree despite the warnings from God, and she gave some of the fruit to Adam. Eve, the spiritual side, became attracted to the benefits of the fruit - being like God. Adam, the physical side, succumbed to the taste, appearance and nourishment it offered. Having eaten of this fruit, their "eyes were opened." Taken literally, it's clear what happened: The serpent convinced the woman that it was good to eat the fruit, which she did, against the will of God. This disobedience was shared by Adam, and the two together have committed the 'original sin.'

But let's return to the spiritual perspective. Perhaps the garden of Eden story is really a description about the challenge every one of us faces in life. Adam and Eve represent the two parts of each human being: the flesh and bones side (Adam) that came from the earth, and the spiritual side (Eve) that came from the breath of life. The serpent approached the Eve-side, because that's where the decision-making happens; the serpent probably would not have gotten too far by speaking directly to Adam, knowing that at the time he was under the complete guidance of the spiritual side.

The very point at which the serpent tempted Eve to eat the fruit is the point when the ego was born in her. Like with Eve, it's when we cross this line that we begin to lose our connection with each other and with God. It's at this point that we think we know the difference between what is 'good' and what is 'evil,' and we begin to walk some very dangerous ground. By 'eating this fruit' we begin to assume that we know what God knows. We shift from a unitive, interconnected mind that enjoys the presence of God (as Adam and Eve did in the garden), to a thought system that begins to label things, attaches judgments to them, begins to categorize things as either good or bad, and as either valuable or worthless. Power becomes more important than people;

personal recognition becomes more important than justice; groups of people are treated collectively based on gender, race, religion, ethnicity, wealth or sexual orientation rather than by their individual integrity, sincerity, sensitivity, or abilities. This arrogance leads to a separation from reality – from the truth. We become distanced from God, and as a result, we distance ourselves from each other. This leaves room for prejudice and bias, which leads to hatred and violence. By eating of this forbidden fruit, what we once were (our true self) does indeed die, just as God warned would happen. It dies in the sense that it begins to get covered up by the characteristics of the dysfunctional ego, with things like attachments, desires, fears, prejudices, and biases. Having eaten of this fruit, Adam and Eve became distanced from God; being fearful they attempted to hide from Him. Their old selves had died.

Now let's take a closer look at the serpent. Initially, Adam and Eve had no thought to even go near the tree of the knowledge of good and evil. They, like the true self in all of us, would naturally obey God's command simply because that's in their nature. There had to be an instigator to disrupt this arrangement, a catalyst for this infraction of God's command. Without a troublemaker, all would be well in the garden. In a metaphorical sense, the serpent represents the unbridled thinking brain. It's the little voice in our head that begins to argue with us, to rationalize or compensate, to use any number of defense mechanisms, or to urge us to satisfy our instincts and drives beyond what's natural. That's the dysfunctional ego. When we yield to the arguments and persuasions of a runaway ego, we begin to run into trouble. A dysfunctional ego veils our true self, and creates a separation from our very soul.

IT STARTS WITH DESIRE

The tree of knowledge of good and evil represents all the desires and attachments to the glitter and falsehood of man's world. It represents the desire to go beyond what we were intended to be, to assume greater importance and worth in relation to others and to nature. The temptations to eat of this fruit come from our present day serpent – the social programming that we grow up with and are faced with every day in the marketplace and media: a false sense of success, the idea that competition is more important than collaboration, that power is more important than people, or that money is more important than life itself. Harmful desires spring from lies told to us by a dysfunctional society. When our ego convinces us to believe these lies, our true selves 'die.' We become separated from God, and this is what "sin" is all about – being in a state of separation from God. Aldous Huxley affirms this by stating:

> "The vast majority of human beings believe that their own selfness and the objects around them possess a reality in themselves, wholly independent of God. This belief leads them to identify their being with their sensations, cravings, and private notions, and in its turn this self-identification with what they are not effectively walls them off from divine influence and the very possibility of deliverance."[14]

The price we pay for the separation from God is the death of the true self. A person in this state now lives in a different world, a world of illusion that is designed to perpetuate this deception.

6 The World of the Dysfunctional Ego

"The condition of alienation, of being asleep, of being unconscious, is the condition of the normal man. Society highly values its normal man. It educates children to lose themselves and to become absurd, and thus to be normal."
R. D. Laing, *The Politics of Experience*

"Our estrangement from each other and from God is the symptom of our fallenness, of our failure to live by the norms embodied by Jesus." Seth Farber, *Unholy Madness: The Church's Surrender to Psychiatry*

THE INDIVIDUAL EGO

The ego naturally tries to convince us that it should manage our life; it will argue that it can offer us a better way to live – to give us a life in tune with the world of man. Many people fall for this attractive argument. Eve fell for it, and so did Adam. As a result they lost their connections with God. Allowing the ego to take over affects us in the same way. The notion of "me" develops into a life of its own, and the idea of "us" diminishes. The result is our inability to see and understand our true connectedness with God and with everything around us. We get lost.

The longer we continue in this state of separation, believing that we are independent, self-capable individuals, the more we start to feel alone. Loneliness leads to fear, a key motivator for the dysfunctional ego – fear that it won't survive, grow, or keep its identity. The ego responds to this fear by using defense mechanisms to protect itself; it soon learns to use prejudices, biases, judgments, false beliefs and blaming. We see this happening in Eden.

ENCOUNTER IN EDEN

Remember that the birth of the dysfunctional ego occurred when Adam and Eve chose to accept the arguments of their thinking brain, represented in the story by the serpent. They began to identify with their thinking brain and thereby became separated from God. The split was made, and then they hid from God in the garden, driven by the guilt of their action. Instead of being a friend of God, they became afraid of Him. Two drivers of the dysfunctional ego, guilt and fear, were in full play.

> "They heard the sound of the Lord God walking in the garden at the time of the evening breeze, and the man and his wife hid themselves from the presence of the Lord God among the trees of the garden. But the Lord God called to the man, and said to him, 'Where are you?' Adam said, 'I heard the sound of you in the garden, and I was afraid, because I was naked; and I hid myself.'" (Genesis 3:8-10)

God immediately knew that they had eaten from the tree that He commanded them not to eat. He could tell that the ego was gaining control because Adam and Eve behaved differently. They weren't themselves. They were now hiding from their guilt, something they didn't have to do previously. When confronted, the nature of the ego is to defend itself, to fight for survival. In the Eden story the ego fought by trying to shift the blame:

> "He said, 'Who told you that you were naked? Have you eaten from the tree of which I commanded you not to eat?' The man said, 'The woman whom you gave to be with me, she gave me the fruit from the tree, and I ate.' Then the Lord God said to the woman, 'What is this that

you have done?' The woman said, 'The serpent tricked me, and I ate.' " (Genesis 3:11-13)

Adam pointed to Eve and said that she was to blame; Eve pointed to the serpent and said that it was to blame. Regardless of blame, everyone involved suffers the consequences of their actions. We can choose our behavior, but we can't choose the consequences of that behavior.

"The Lord God said to the serpent, 'Because you have done this, cursed are you among all animals and among all wild creatures; upon your belly you shall go, and dust you shall eat all the days of your life. I will put enmity between you and the woman, and between your offspring and hers; he will strike your head, and you will strike his heel.'" (Genesis 3:14-15)

Without the presence of God, the mind and the soul will always be at odds with each other ("I will put enmity between you and the woman,"), each struggling to gain and maintain control of the person, and this will carry on throughout the generations (...and between your offspring and hers.). Although the last phrase (...he will strike your head, and you will strike his heel) has been used as a reference to Christ battling the devil, we could also imagine that God was addressing both the serpent and the woman together at this point. God noted that the serpent (ego) strikes at the head, the home of the mind, and that the woman (spiritual side) would always be reacting to the ego's attacks, not knowing when they may occur, thereby having to grab at its heel to pull it back. Whatever the case, this passage is a description of the struggle to stay connected with God in our life and the forces that oppose this.

> "To the woman he said, 'I will greatly increase your pangs in childbearing; in pain you shall bring forth children, yet your desire shall be for your husband, and he shall rule over you.' And to the man he said, 'Because you have listened to the voice of your wife, and have eaten of the tree about which I commanded you, You shall not eat of it, cursed is the ground because of you; in toil you shall eat of it all the days of your life; thorns and thistles it shall bring forth for you; and you shall eat the plants of the field. By the sweat of your face you shall eat bread until you return to the ground, for out of you were taken; you are dust, and to dust you shall return.' " (Genesis 3:16-19)

The unbridled ego would be a bane to the soul, and as such the soul would always be threatened by it. The flesh part, Adam, in this disconnected state would toil with sweat on his brow all the days of his life under the reins of a relentless, insatiable ego, and in the end he would return to the ground from whence he came. The dysfunctional ego seeks its own illusionary interests, as though it were the center of the universe, even if it may sometimes cause the destruction of the person it inhabits. It doesn't care. This is the world of the dysfunctional ego, and according to Thomas Merton:

> "This claim to omnipotence, our deepest secret and our inmost shame, is in fact the source of all our sorrows, all our unhappiness, all our dissatisfactions, all our mistakes and deceptions."[15]

DESIRE: SEEDS OF THE EGO

As we saw in the garden of Eden story, the birth of the ego began with a desire. Eve, the soul, was led to believe she could be more like God. She had forgotten *she was already an image of God*, but was convinced by the serpent that there was more for her than what she had. Adam, being the physical part of the package, came along obediently under the influence of the Eve side.

> "For if he who fills his desire on one of the things which he pursues should then incline his desire to something else, he finds himself empty again in that regard. And if he should fill himself on this, he becomes empty and a vacant container once more for something else. And we

never stop doing this until we depart from this material life."

Gregory of Nyssa, *The Life of Moses*

It's important to note that some desires are natural and good. Desires of the soul are those connected with the will of God. These are the desires in us that seek God's love and compassion for all. These are the desires we have for other people to also find their way to self-fulfillment. These are the desires that strive for healing and wellness of self and others, and for economic justice. "Take delight in the Lord, and he will give you the desires of your heart." (Psalm 37:4)

Besides desires of the heart, we may also experience desires generated by natural instincts such as hunger, safety and procreation. The natural desires of the soul and of the body are not sins. It's when we attempt to satisfy any of these natural desires through unnatural means that we begin to run into trouble. It's when the serpent ego provokes us to cross this line that we begin to surrender our true self to the world of illusion. Remember how the devil tempted Jesus in the desert? "He [Jesus] fasted forty days and forty nights, and afterwards he was famished. The tempter came and said to him, 'If you are the Son of God, command these stones to become loaves of bread.'" (Matthew 4:2-3) Jesus, of course, declined this temptation knowing that using his power in this unnatural way would open the door for further trouble. "For when desire goes beyond the limits of lawful need, what else is this than the council of the devil?" says Gregory of Nyssa. Problems begin when the action taken to satisfy a natural desire far outstrip the necessities of life. When a desire is fed too much it often grows into an attachment.

ATTACHMENTS

An attachment is a persistent demand our dysfunctional ego makes to satisfy a specific desire to the point that the obsession becomes part of our identity. An attachment begins as a desire such as the want of a thing, like a new car or house, or it can be the need for a situation, like a powerful job or having a certain person for a spouse or partner. It's no longer just a preference or a fondness for something, but gradually becomes a building block of our personality, being present in almost every conscious moment of our lives. Every decision or circumstance is weighed against the possibility of satisfying this desire. Our true self gets buried under the burdens of these attachments. The original desire, or attraction, generates an illusion of pleasure which, over time, grows into an attachment for the thing or the situation. Why? On the one hand, the fleeting pleasure needs to be repeated because it does not endure. The initial attraction can lead to some pleasure, but not to happiness. It does not sustain itself. The fulfillment and satisfaction that is felt for a while is soon lost, and is followed by a feeling of boredom and weariness, leading one to seek repeated and stronger attractions. On the other hand a fear develops that the thing desired or owned may be lost, so the person spends an increasing amount of time and energy on activities to guarantee its survival. These two forces, desire and fear, now ensure that the attachment becomes a driving force in the person's life and will influence the choices that are made in every moment.

Every attachment becomes a veil that covers our true self in some way. Every attachment discolors our thinking ability and closes us off from the present moment, the only place where real life can be found. One psalmist complains of a dysfunctional ego grown so large that he or she can no longer perceive the truth: "For evils have encompassed me without number; my iniquities have overtaken me until I can not see; they are more than the hairs of my head, and my heart fails me." (Psalm 40:12)   The cycle of desire to attachment continues and gradually "hardens the heart."

> "A man has many skins in himself, covering the depths of his heart. Man knows too many things; he does not know himself. Why, thirty or forty skins or hides, just like an ox's or a bear's, so thick and hard, cover the soul."
>
> Meister Eckhart

Veil after veil is added over the heart. Over time, they pile up higher and higher until the light of the true soul can no longer shine through to the outside world.

> "The soul that is attached to anything, however much good there may be in it, will not arrive at the liberty of divine union. For whether it be a strong rope or a slender and delicate thread that holds the bird, it matters not, if it really holds it fast; for, until the cord be broken, the bird cannot fly. So the soul, held by the bonds of human affections, however slight they may be, cannot, while they last, make its way to God."   St. John of the Cross

Remember Jesus' saying about a rich person? "Jesus said to his disciples, 'Truly I tell you, it will be hard for a rich person to enter the kingdom of heaven. Again I tell you, it is easier for a camel to go through the eye of a needle than for someone who is rich to enter the kingdom of God.' " (Matthew 19:23-24) It's not the wealth of a person that will keep him or her from experiencing the presence of God – it's the attachment to that wealth that blocks the person from connecting to God. The rich person may put more importance on the preservation and growth of money than on keeping his or her soul connected with the Creator who gave life. Losing his connection to the kingdom, the person lives a life that isn't true.

Gradually we will find ourselves more and more separated from our true self, and our peace diminishes. The nature and strength of attachments are described by Gregory of Nyssa:

> "Now the soul is in some way attached to the pleasant things in life through the senses of the body. Through the eyes it delights in material beauty, through the ears it inclines to melodious sounds, and so it is also affected by smell, taste, and touch, as nature has disposed to be proper to each. Hence, as it is attached to the pleasant things of life through the sensible faculty as if by a nail, it is hard to turn away from them. It has grown up together with these attachments much

the same way as the shellfish and snails are bound to their covering of clay; and so it is slow to make such movements, since it drags along the whole burden of a lifetime. As such is its condition, the soul is easily captured by its persecutors with the threat of confiscation of property or loss of some other things that are coveted in this life; and so it gives in easily, and yields to the power of its persecutor." [16]

Attachments are the building blocks of ego-identity. They become very important to the ego, and the ego will go to great lengths to feed these attachments.

EGO FOOD

The dysfunctional ego has bottomless needs, feeling that it's never good enough, never has the right things to satisfy it. It has unnatural needs that demand to be filled in unnatural ways. Whether it tends to overinflate its own importance, or undervalue itself, it does so relative to what it believes other people think of it. The ego's strength comes from an illusion, a perception it has of how other people view it and evaluate it. The ego believes that other people spend a lot of time thinking and talking about it. The truth of the matter, however, is well-described in a passage about Tess from *Tess of the D'Urbervilles*:

> "She might have seen that what had bowed her head so profoundly – the thought of the world's concern at her situation – was founded on an illusion. She was not an existence, an experience, a passion, a structure of sensations, to anybody but herself. To all humankind Tess was only a passing thought. Even to friends she was no more than a frequently passing thought. If she made herself miserable the livelong night and day it was only this much to them – 'Ah, she makes herself unhappy.' If she tried to be cheerful, to dismiss all care, to take pleasure in the daylight, the flowers, the baby, she could only be this idea to them – 'Ah, she bears it very well.'"[17]

The ego's existence is anchored in the past and in the future. It cannot survive in the present moment. The egoic mind (the state of a person with a dysfunctional ego) is primarily conditioned by the interpretation of past events as well as its worry and fear about the future.

Another thing about dysfunctional egos is that they tend to identify more with roles we have in life than with the service that these roles provide (the functions of those roles). For example, "I am a doctor" versus "I help people get well." Or, "I am a corporate executive" versus

"I help a group of people achieve a task that helps others." The identification with role versus function happens because the ego is hungry for identity, particularly as it relates to others in social contexts; its sense of worth is relative to other people's position and importance. It tries to continually make an impression on others, demanding undue attention. The ego strengthens itself by complaining about others so that its own status is elevated. It grows best when it can "put down" others. It thrives on the conflict it can create so that it feels more alive. It confuses facts with opinions and popularity.

DEFENSE MECHANISMS

The aim of the ego is self-preservation and growth. To preserve its identity and respond to its fears, the dysfunctional ego will employ any number of defense mechanisms such as denial, displacement, projection, rationalization, suppression, and regression, to name a few. We saw this happen in the garden of Eden with the blaming game.

Oddly, sometimes the ego identifies with its own suffering, its own unfortunate situation, and will use these defense mechanisms to preserve its own suffering-identity. Some egos thrive on this self-abasement. "I'm not good enough." "I'll never be anything." "Nothing good will ever happen to me." "I'm too ugly to have a friend." This variety of ego thrives on low self-esteem based on an illusion that is just as misplaced as the one used by an overinflated ego. It will thrive on this unhappy identification simply because it's the clearest form of identification it has developed. The removal of its own suffering-identity would be more painful than keeping it, especially if it's fearful about whom or what it would become after the suffering was removed. It therefore goes to great lengths to cling to all it knows – the comfort of its own suffering.

Feeling superior or inferior to someone else is entirely the dysfunctional ego at work. Either way, dysfunctional egos are damaging and hurtful to a person; building an illusion that can not be supported by reality. The ego loves identification and a separate existence; it abhors connectedness and unity. The separateness created by the ego is what brings eventual suffering. This is the world of the individual ego. But what happens when two or more egos get together and feed off of each other?

THE COLLECTIVE EGO

Egos tend to attract other egos when they discover a common cause to further themselves or their agenda. These alliances, although fueled by individual agendas, grow strong as they begin to form a "collective ego." They begin to discover common norms and values that further solidify their union. They realize that by being together they reinforce a specific kind of ideal or cause, even though it's also an illusion. In most cases these groups get no further than occasional social clubs or cliques. Some may take on a greater presence, such as street gangs. They begin to see themselves as warriors against the world that threatens their existence or ideals (versus joining together to battle some injustice). Still others grow into nation states. These, as history has shown, can get out of hand and cause great harm, especially when they grow a hatred for a specific group of people. National collectives can become deluded about their power and righteousness, overtly coercing their residents with slogans like, "Our country: love it or leave it." Consider Stephen Decatur's famous toast, "Our country... may she always be in the right;

but our country, right or wrong!" Although this is designed to stimulate a sense of patriotism in the minds of listeners, it also opens the doorway for the serpent of Eden to form a collective ego in our minds that replaces the way of God.

TWO WORLDS APART

The rise of the collective ego begins to shape a world of its own based on a special set of values that help it survive and grow. It uses a system that seeks an illusionary appearance of fairness for all, but actually only rewards those who know how to use the system best. It makes a world that displays the virtues of its ingenuity and progress while hiding the underlying corruption and deterioration of society and nature. The differences between the world of egos and the world of God are the subject of much scripture because this is a very important message God is trying to get across to us. Here are a few selections from the Hebrew Scriptures, the Gospels and the epistles:

> "For my thoughts are not your thoughts, nor are your ways my ways, says the Lord. For as the heavens are higher than the earth, so are my

ways higher than your ways and my thoughts than your thoughts." (Isaiah 55:8-9)

"Do not store up for yourselves treasures on earth, where moth and rust consume and where thieves break in and steal; but store up for yourselves treasures in heaven, where neither moth nor rust consumes and where thieves do not break in and steal. For where your treasure is, there your heart will be also." (Matthew 6:19-21)

"For those who want to save their life will lose it, and those who lose their life for my sake will find it. For what will it profit them if they gain the whole world but forfeit their life? Or what will they give in return for their life?" (Matthew 16:25-26)

"No slave can serve two masters; for a slave will either hate the one and love the other, or be devoted to the one and despise the other. You cannot serve God and wealth.' The Pharisees, who were lovers of money, heard all this, and they ridiculed him. So he said to them, "You are those who justify yourselves in the sight of others; but God knows your hearts; for what is prized by human beings is an abomination in the sight of God." (Luke 16:13-15)

"Peace I leave with you; my peace I give you. I do not give to you as the world gives. Do not let your hearts be troubled, and do not let them be afraid." (John 14:27)

"For those who live according to the flesh [physical world] set their minds on the things of the flesh, but those who live according to the spirit set their minds on the things of the spirit."
(Romans 8:5)

"For the wisdom of this world is foolishness with God. For it is written, 'He catches the wise in the craftiness,' and again, 'The Lord knows the thoughts of the wise, that they are futile.'"
(1 Corinthians 3:19-21)

"Do not love the world or the things of the world. The love of the Father is not in those who love the world; for all that is in the world – the desire of the flesh, the desire of the eyes, the pride in riches – comes not from the Father but from the world. And the world and its desire are passing away, but those who do the will of God live forever." (1 John 2:15-17)

THE SERPENT TODAY: PROGRAMMING

The world of collective egos uses cultural and social programming to achieve its ends. Programming is the process by which outside influences shape our thought patterns which result in a predictable, targeted set of behaviors. The aim of programming is to shape thought and behavior. It's the sum total of the experiences we are exposed to in our everyday environment. Programming comes from our parents, teachers, friends, pastors, television, books, movies, and the Internet, to name a few. Some programming is designed to help people to become who they were meant to be, but other programming is designed to bring a person's life into alignment with a specific collective thought and behavior, which is, quite frankly, evil. This type of programming is designed to further the power and control of some individual, group or cause that is, in reality, a dysfunctional collective ego. Programming is a key tool of the collective ego.

Constructive programming, on the other hand, can sometimes be called training, formation, or spiritual direction, and can come in the form of support groups, teachers or counselors. This type of programming is usually quite forthright and honest, and deals with the present moment – not so much with the past or the future. A person's heart, free from dysfunctional encumbrances, will be able to tell the intent of the programming.

Harmful programming is much more subtle, but also much more prevalent. It relies heavily on using guilt of the past, or shame and fear of the future. It's designed to nurture the person's dysfunctional ego, feeding it and making it stronger so that it controls the heart and directs the mind to make certain pre-determined decisions. Collectively, the messages it offers create norms that define our culture and turn falsehoods into "pseudo-facts" through sheer prominence. Malicious programming grows harmful beliefs, ideas, habits, attachments, fears, biases, prejudices, etc.

The collective egos today are numerous and powerful. They want you to give up control of your life and become part of them. They misuse the gifts of communication and persuasion to support their causes, not caring much about individuals becoming who they were meant to be. How, then, do we reclaim our natural spiritual birthright? How do we shed the scales of the ego from our eyes like Saul did on his journey to Damascus? (Acts 9) We cannot fight directly against the dysfunctional ego, individual or collective, and win. The key is to bring the light of awareness, the light of consciousness to it. This is the Light of Truth. This is the Truth that will set you free.   .

7 Awakening

"Sleeper, awake! Rise from the dead, and Christ will shine on you." (Ephesians 5:14b)

"Besides this, you know what time it is, how it is now the moment for you to wake from sleep. For salvation is nearer to us now than when we became believers;" (Romans 13:11)

"Unless nature finds a way of transcending itself by means of itself, we are lost." Aldous Huxley, *The Perennial Philosophy*

Our personal survival, and that of mankind, rests with our ability to awaken to the serpent in our lives. Unless we reclaim the spiritual heritage given to us in the garden of Eden, we are destined to repeat the mistakes of the past. If we continue to be guided by our dysfunctional egos, insisting that we're independent creatures above the laws and love of nature, we will continue to fail. But if we return to the Tree of Life, reconnecting with God, with each other, and with nature, we will find the path back to Eden. How can we do this?

RECLAIMING EDEN

St. Paul writes that there is nothing that can separate us from the love of God: "For I am convinced that neither death, nor life, nor angels, nor rulers, nor things present, nor things to come, nor powers, nor height, nor depth, nor anything else in all creation, will be able to separate us from the love of God in Christ Jesus our Lord." (Romans 8:38-39). We see in numerous places in the Hebrew Scriptures, the New Testament and many world religions that God is drawn to us as much as we are to Him. As we learned in earlier chapters, this is because we are made in His image. We are part of Him, and someday He will bring each of us back home to Him in a state of grace, bringing us all back together again. How He will do this is beyond our comprehension. But the message of full redemption and salvation of all God's children is first seen late in the third chapter of Genesis. It has been consistently overlooked, but it's there if we look closely:

"The man named his wife Eve, because she was the mother of all living. And the Lord God made garments of skins for the man and for his wife, and clothed them. Then the Lord God said, 'See, the man has become like one of us, knowing good and evil; and now, he might reach out his hand and take also from the tree of life, and eat, and live forever' – Therefore the Lord God sent him forth from the garden of Eden, to till the ground from which he was taken. He drove out the man; and at the east of the garden of Eden he placed the cherubim, and a sword flaming and turning to guard the way to the tree of life." (Genesis 3:20-24)

Even though mankind was on the verge of being expelled from the garden, we see acts of love and compassion. Adam names his wife "Eve", because she was to be the mother of all living. The man knew that it would be through the feminine side, Eve, from who future life would spring forth; not only physical life, but spiritual awakening and rebirth as well. It would be through Eve that the Light would eventually come to us all to awaken all those who had fallen asleep under the power of the false-self, the serpent ego.

A SURPRISE VERDICT

God's concern at this point in the story appears to be that since man failed to exercise his free will properly (turning it over to the forces of his ego, i.e., the serpent), he might also eat of the tree of life, and live forever in this now imperfect state. Man greatly overstepped his bounds. But this is the risk that comes with free will, the key ingredient that makes love possible. God is willing to take the risk with each one of us because we're worth it. But because man misused his free will, he could not remain in the garden reaping the garden's benefits – he was not ready for the gifts God wanted to give him. Man separated himself from the presence of God (but remember that God never separates Himself from man!). Man had to leave the garden until he would one day be ready to live the life he was supposed to live. But he would not be gone forever – God would pursue him until he was ready to return.

As Irenaeus of Lyons explains in *Against Heresies,*

> "That is why God drove them out of paradise and carried them off far away from the tree of life. It was not because he refused them this tree out of jealousy, as some have had the audacity to maintain. No, it was because he acted out of compassion in order that human beings might not remain transgressors for ever, that the sin with which they found themselves burdened might not be immortal, that the evil should not be without end and therefore without remedy. God therefore halted them in their transgression

by interposing death...by setting them a term through the dissolution of the flesh which would take place in the earth, in order that human beings, by 'dying to sin', should begin one day to 'live as God.'"[18]

The banishment from the garden was not done out of jealousy, but was done for man's own sake. The road back to spiritual wholeness, to awakening, would have to be accomplished in the outside world. The conditions needed for man to regain his own true self and shed the power of the serpent ego would not be found within the garden grounds. Gregory Nazianzen offers a similar perspective:

"God placed man in paradise – whatever this paradise was – and gave him freedom, in order that happiness of the beneficiary might be as great as that of the benefactor. He bade him watch over immortal plants, possibly divine thoughts...He gave him a law to exercise his freedom. This law was a commandment: he might pick the fruit of some trees, and one that he might not touch. This tree was the tree of knowledge. God had not planted it originally for the undoing of man and it was not out of jealousy that God forbade him to go near it – let not the enemies of God intervene here,... For that tree was, to my mind, the tree of contemplation, which only those could enter into without harm whose spiritual preparation had reached sufficient perfection."[19]

Gregory Nazianzen goes on to explain that man was expelled from the garden because he was not spiritually mature enough to handle it; he was not yet ready for it. But this also implies that at some point man would, and could, be ready for it. God would one day bring us all home.

In the final verses of the third chapter of Genesis we see God implementing His verdict. "He drove out the man; and at the east of the garden of Eden he placed the cherubim, and a sword flaming and turning to guard the way to the tree of life." (Genesis 3:24).

There is something in this final verse that is crucial to our understanding. Let's look at this carefully. The tree of life was not forbidden to Adam when he was in the garden before "the Fall." Since he yielded to the serpent ego, however, he was no longer able to enjoy the fruits of the tree of life. Like Adam and Eve, while we're under the dominion of our dysfunctional egos access to the gifts of the Holy Spirit (love, joy, peace, patience, kindness, generosity, faithfulness, gentleness, and self-control) are hard to accept or realize. We just cannot have it both ways. When we become separated from God we become separated from His gifts. They are still there, being offered to us continuously; we just can't see them.

One of the most striking things about this passage, however, is that Adam, the man, was *the only one expelled from the garden!* Eve was not. Let's read this verse carefully again: "He drove out the *man*..." The Hebrew text is quite clear. It does not say that they were both driven out, or that the man and his wife were driven out, or that mankind was driven out. It simply says that *the man* was driven out.

On the surface this verdict seems grossly unfair. Why was the man banished from the garden, but the woman was not? After all, didn't this all start with her? Since Adam represents the physical side of us, his banishment from the garden is a clear message that no amount of physical effort, logic or reasoning of the mind will regain access to the garden and the tree of life. The physical side isn't equipped to overcome the power of the dysfunctional ego which blocks our path back to Eden. We cannot fight the ego directly and expect to win. The only way we can reclaim Eden will be through Eve – the spiritual side of us. It is the soul that has the power to awaken and dissolve the dysfunctional ego if and only if it's connected to our higher power. It is the Light that will dissolve the ego, not reasoning or physical power.

> "Jesus answered. 'Very truly, I tell you, no one can enter the kingdom of God without being born of water and Spirit. What is born of the flesh is flesh, and what is born of the Spirit is spirit.' " (John 3:5-6)

And,

> "It is the spirit that gives life; the flesh is useless." (John 6:63)

Here is a critical point: we need to keep in mind the two different parts of our humanness: the spiritual side where free will resides, and the physical side, home of the mind and birthplace of the dysfunctional ego. While the mind is a tool that collects, stores and processes information, judgment and moral choice are functions of the soul. The decision to identify with the ego was made by the spiritual side, but it's also the side that would eventually have to dissolve the dysfunctional ego and reunite with God. The body and the mind will follow along once this decision has been made. The body, mind and soul would once again be in harmony.

Eve, the breath of life, was not banned from the garden. She still had access to the riches of the

Kingdom because she is the part of us that connects directly with God. The way back to Eden is through our soul side. Adam and Eve, as two sides of one person, would be shown the way back to Eden over the ensuing years. Their lives, and our lives outside the garden, would gradually bring us to a level of spiritual maturity that would one day free us of the serpent ego and allow us once again to be who we were meant to be. Each of us would then serve God from our heart, and not our head, in our own unique and special way. This journey involves both a primary purpose in life (our awakening) and a secondary purpose (our uniqueness in serving God).

OUR PRIMARY (INNER) PURPOSE

Our primary, inner purpose, therefore, is the same for every person – to "wake up," to become aware of the dysfunctional ego within us, the tempter, and its desire to completely take over our thoughts and lives. Awakening to this situation is to realize that the true self is the core of our being; it's the image of God given to us. It's where free will choices are made, and from where our uniqueness will flow out into the world as part of the interdependent body of Christ. Awakening is to realize that the mind isn't a bad thing, but is a tool to be used for its intended purpose – to gather, store, and process information; to regulate body functions and physical activity. Awakening is to realize that we're a part of a huge spiritual network that connects us to each other, to God, and to the world. Awakening is to realize that we're eternal beings in a temporal body. Awakening is to realize that the Kingdom of God is within us and all around us. Awakening is to bring a fresh consciousness to our lives.

The serpent ego is the craftiest of all creatures we will ever encounter, but it *can* be tamed. It's very much a separate entity taking on a life and existence all its own. It wants to survive and grow, but the only way it can do that is by getting us to believe it and accept it as being real. It wants us to fully identify with it and adopt it as being our real self. If we believe it, we disconnect ourselves from God; we become separated from Him and from each other. If we awaken to it, we open the gates to the love and compassion of God that are there waiting for us.

8 Spiritual Postures

"And what I say to you I say to all: keep awake." (Mark 13:37)

"We must not wish anything other than what happens from moment to moment, all the while, however, exercising ourselves in goodness."
St. Catherine of Genoa

"Direct knowledge of God cannot be had except by union, and union can be achieved only be the annihilation of the self-regarding ego, which is the barrier separating you from God."
Aldous Huxley, *The Perennial Philosophy*

To be fully awakened has been called *puritas cordis*, or purity of heart, by the church Fathers. It's the true self, the soul, unfettered by the bonds of a dysfunctional ego, living a life that it was meant to live. This is our objective, this is enlightenment. Enlightenment isn't something only to be achieved by a select few, but it's the natural state for all of us, given to us in Eden.

The awakening process can be facilitated by using five key techniques discussed below. These techniques are spiritual "postures" that we can take as we travel through each moment of the day. The spiritual postures are attitudes and positions of *consciousness* that are centered in the soul. These five postures will be discussed in the sequence that they generally occur in the awakening process:

1) Ego Awareness

2) Present Moment Awareness

3) Acceptance

4) Detachment

5) Presence of God

It is important to remember that spiritual development isn't a solitary journey. We do it together. Depending on the strength of your ego, you may need professional assistance in applying these spiritual postures. In any case, we all need to have a team of supporters around us: friends, counselors, pastors and spiritual directors. Find those people who have your interest in mind and work with them.

SPIRITUAL POSTURE 1 –

EGO AWARENESS

The first thing that has to happen in the process of awakening is for us to have some change in consciousness. There has to be a realization, either sudden or gradual, that our behavior and thoughts are not really who we are or who we want to be. We may realize that we are "not our true self," or that we are "beside ourselves." There is often a sudden awareness that there are actually two entities struggling for control of our consciousness. This realization has been called a shift in consciousness or the initial point of awakening. This is the time when we recognize that we have been under the influence of the egoic mind (the dysfunctional ego) and we need to break free. We understand that there needs to be a separation of ourselves from our thought processes. It's a disidentification with the mind. The goal isn't to get rid of the thinking mind, but to put it back into its proper position relative to the soul. This is spiritual posture 1 – ego awareness. Eckhart Tolle emphasizes this by writing:

"The greatest achievement of humanity is not its works of art, science or technology, but the recognition of its own dysfunction, its own madness."[21]

Ego awareness begins by understanding and being aware of the actions of the serpent ego as they occur or are about to occur. Being *aware* of what is happening when we come under the influence of the serpent is one of the biggest steps in taming it. With a little practice, we can see and feel when the ego moves in. What are some of the symptoms of its impending approach? Any of the following *could* be a sign that our true self, the self that is connected with God, is being threatened:

- Fear
- Anger
- Shame
- Bias
- Greed
- Envy
- Gossip
- Irritation

- Worry
- Guilt
- Prejudice
- Lust
- Confusion
- Hatred
- Anxiousness
- Restlessness

Any behavior that diminishes us, other people, creatures, nature or property is probably a good indication of the presence of a dysfunctional ego. Because our dysfunctional ego isn't really part of our true self, we can gain an advantage over it by recognizing it as being separate from us. We can begin to distance ourselves from the serpent ego by observing, in the moment, how we're feeling, how we're behaving, how we're reacting to other persons or situations. To begin to create this separation from our ego, we can ask ourselves questions such as:

"Why did I say that?"

"What am I feeling about that right now?"

"How would I describe what just happened to me?"

These and similar self-examining questions help us to begin to separate ourselves from our dysfunctional ego. Our true selves would not have behaved poorly, but while we're under the spell and control of the ego, we behaved in a way that will either protect our ego from threats or that manipulated other people to help our own ego grow and thrive.

So we begin to separate ourselves (the 'observer') from the feeling or action (the 'observed'). When we first practice this technique, we may not be able to remember to ask these questions of ourselves until later. We may have to begin by taking some time at the end of the day to reflect on the events of the day. This can help us to begin developing the skill of being an observer of our own feelings and reactions. Journaling is one way to do this.

Perhaps something happened during the day to make you feel slighted or angry. There are a couple of ways to reflect on the incident. The first begins with writing the phrase in your journal, "I was angry because so-and-so said this to me." This approach shows that you have *identified* with your anger – the serpent ego and you are one. Someone attacked your dysfunctional ego, so *you* are angry.

The other way keeps us in a better position, and begins to pry the serpent's coils from around our soul, allowing the power of God to begin to flow back through our true self. In this approach we would begin by writing, "I *felt* anger because so-and-so said this to me." We have now placed the anger out in front of our self where it can be examined more carefully. We will soon discover that our dysfunctional ego was injured by the incident, not our true self. As soon as we realize this, the anger dissipates because it's exposed for what it really is. It can't stand against the light of truth. Our true self can't be harmed by the words fired at us from another person's ego (remember that *their* true self would never say such a thing!). We realize that the incident was an ego-to-ego exchange, the other person's ego was protecting itself by trying to diminish our ego. The true selves of the people weren't even involved. They were buried under tons of serpent scales.

So, here is the subtle, yet all-important difference:

"I *feel* anger;" versus "I *am* angry."

"I *feel* frustrated;" versus "I *am* frustrated."

"I *feel* fear;" versus "I *am* afraid."

This technique can be a great tool to realize that we can separate our self from our ego feelings. This creates ego awareness. This separation will begin to show us that in most cases it's our ego that has been hurt and not us. This will allow us to have more compassion for our self, *and* for the other person who may be totally unaware that his or her dysfunctional ego is in control of him or her. Incidents of the day that used to really upset us can now be an opportunity for further learning and spiritual growth. These incidents are no longer assaults, but gifts! They teach us more about our self and our dysfunctional ego that's now on the way to dissolving. Don't resist them or renounce them, just observe them.

This begins the process of reclaiming our soul, our connection with God. Eckhart Tolle said:

> "The single most important step in your journey toward enlightenment is this: learn to disidentify from your mind. Create gaps in the stream of the mind."[21]

As you practice this technique, eventually you will be able to create this ego awareness closer and closer to the actual incident itself. You won't need to wait until the end of the day to realize that the feelings that have arisen in you are the result of a wounded ego, and not your true self. Eventually you catch the ego before it has a chance to act.

Rarely in life, except in emergencies where danger is imminent, do we have to respond as quickly as we think we must. There is usually time to think before we respond. But cultural conditioning often demands an immediate response in many situations. Pausing to think and craft an appropriate response is generally viewed poorly as a sign of dullness or a product of low intelligence, or of being unprepared in a fast-paced society. "Time is money," "If you snooze, you lose," and other slogans remind us not to waste time, even a moment, or you'll get behind and start to lose ground.

But this is short-term thinking, invented by egos, the kind of thinking that often gets us into big trouble. The truth is that if we take more time up front than the "fast thinker," the person who is good at "thinking on their feet," we end up better off in the long run. Taking time to process and make good decisions creates fewer mistakes, strengthens relationships, and generally improves the quality of life. Pausing pays off in many ways! The soul is not in a hurry. The ego is in a race.

It's only through awareness, and not just thinking, that we come to learn the difference between fact and illusion. Illusions belong to our ego and not to the real self. Illusions will diminish when we bring them into the light of awareness, the light of truth. Once we have space between our true self and illusions, we will be able to respond appropriately to the situation at hand.

SPIRITUAL POSTURE 2 –

PRESENT MOMENT AWARENESS

Once we have become aware of our ego, we can begin to look at each moment of our lives differently. The awareness developed to see our own dysfunctional ego can now be turned outward to the world around us.

Each moment of life can now be viewed with fresh perspective. This is spiritual posture 2 – present moment awareness.

The present moment is that little bit of time and space that exists between the past and the future. It's what is happening right now at this very moment. The present moment isn't as long as a day, an hour, or even a minute. It's a continuous flow of very short time segments through the space around you, within your field of awareness.

Consider any action, such as walking. As you walk, think of every single step you take as being the present moment. The last step you took is already in the past, and the next step you take is still in the future, even though it's just moments away. The most important step you take is the one you are taking right now, this very moment.

> "Time is measured by a threefold division, past, present and future... If you consider the present, it is through Him [God] that you live; you, however, are master only of the present."
> Gregory of Nyssa, *The Lord's Prayer*

The challenge we face with the present moment is that although our bodies and souls live in the present moment, our egos thrive on the past and the future.

Egos cannot survive in the present moment. They cannot survive in the light of awareness and truth. They thrive on the pain of the past and the worries of the future. This is what gives them their identity.

Consider the walk we are taking. We may see an obstacle ahead of us which may generate concern or fear, or we may remember how we stepped on someone else's toes a few steps ago (carrying from the past guilt or the shame of our clumsiness). The warning of the danger ahead or the memory of the past event becomes part of our ego's identity in the present moment. The ego uses these events to affirm its illusions about life and the necessity for it to maintain control. How we deal with these past and future images in the present moment makes them either debilitating baggage or benevolent gifts. They will either block our sense of the present moment and our connection with God (thereby feeding the ego), or they will be used to develop a better understanding of ourselves and others (thereby reestablishing our connection with God).

The present moment is the only period of time when we're truly conscious. If we're thinking about the past or the future, then we're not truly conscious to life. The connection we make with God and to His kingdom only happens now, in the present moment. As Anthony de Mello writes:

> "To find the Kingdom is the easiest thing in the world, but it is also the most difficult. It is easy because the Kingdom is all around you, and within you, and all you have to do is reach out and take possession of it. It is difficult because if you wish to possess it you may possess nothing else."[22]

Present moment awareness holds the key to enlightenment, to releasing us from the grasp of the dysfunctional ego. Spiritual consciousness brings us this light of awareness; consciousness is only possible in the present moment – not in the past or the future.

Present moment awareness is the key to living a full life. It's the essence of being. Everything real that happens to us happens in the present moment. Our connection with God only occurs in the present. Our connection with others and with the earth only occurs in the present. Our presence in the present moment links us into the field of all possibilities; it's where we connect into the spiritual Internet, allowing our prayer power to flow out to others, and where we receive the flow of love and blessings.

Living in the present moment does not mean we forget the past or ignore the future. What it means is that we use these other two time frames in the proper way. Our past experiences are great teachers, and we must learn from them. But we avoid dwelling on them to the point that they interfere with our present moment. Planning for the future is important, too, but the steps to get to the future all happen in the present moment, one at a time. Now is when the future is made.

How can we live in the present moment? The first of two techniques is to practice spiritual posture 1 – ego awareness, to become the observer of our thoughts and how we're spending our time. This will alert us to when we're not in the present moment. By catching our self dwelling on the past or the future, we immediately return to the present moment. The ego disappears and our true self is able to function freely.

The other key technique involves becoming more aware of the physical world around us. It's using our five senses with intentionality. We go slowly through each moment of life with the curiosity of a child, noticing things around us. Jesus said, "Truly I tell you, unless you change and become like children, you will never enter the kingdom of heaven." (Matthew 18:3) This awareness includes paying attention to our own breathing, or feeling the movement of our limbs as we walk, or watching the flight of a bird, or seeing all the shades of a color where before we thought we saw only one. Listen for the voice of God in the wind, and in the words of another person. Feel the grass or the leaf of a plant. Treat objects as sacred gifts of God. Look at people as temples of God. Consider each of your movements as a sacrament to God.

SPIRITUAL POSTURE 3 –

ACCEPTANCE

Awareness of the existence of our ego opens the way for us to accept who we really are and the situation we find ourselves in. We come to realize that almost all of the struggles we have with ourselves have come from either our own ego or from the ego of other people. Acceptance is an important piece for our spiritual journey as it allows more of the light of truth into our lives.

Acceptance of who we are and where we are in life means that we accept our present situation and condition for whatever it is at the moment, without attaching any labels to it, such as good or bad. We don't argue with what is, because that will have absolutely no value in changing it. Resisting the present moment actually returns power back to our ego, which is never satisfied to begin with. We lose our grasp on the present moment when we attempt to renounce, resist or refuse to accept the present moment and our place in it. The simple phrase "It is what it is," helps us to remember that each moment is a result of all the previous moments that led up to it – a result of many more things than we could ever control. So, there is little point in arguing about what exists in this moment.

Acceptance is the spiritual posture we take *within ourselves* relative to who we are, or what is happening in the moment we find ourselves in. It's not necessarily the outward posture we take when there are situations that are clearly not tolerable or where there is imminent threat to life or property. We don't outwardly accept, for example, living in an abusive situation, cruelty to animals, or staying in the path of an oncoming storm. These are things where action must be taken. But, the action taken will be most effective if we avoid labeling it, judging it, or losing our true sense of self as we act. We must act from the soul and not the ego.

Acceptance is not passive. We acknowledge the moment for what it is, and accept who we are at this moment in time. Acceptance of the moment releases opportunities that would otherwise be invisible. Acceptance of the moment allows us to gain the best understanding of a situation without the interference of past baggage or future worry.

"Accept whatever comes to you woven in the pattern of your destiny, for what could more aptly meet your needs?" Marcus Aurelius

Once we have accepted the totality of the moment for what it is, we can effectively choose the proper course of action. Usually there are only three choices. We can either:

1) Change the situation; or

2) Leave the situation for something different; or

3) Accept the situation if we can not change it or leave it.

Failure to do any of these three will result in suffering, which, I suppose, is actually a fourth choice many people take.

Acceptance is our realization that our true self is made in the image of God, and that He accepts us as He made us. This doesn't mean we're finished growing, that we have "arrived." It does mean, however, that we are where we are supposed to be at this moment, and all the resistance, non-acceptance, judgment by us or others is totally useless in helping us along. God is our judge and guide, and He is the only one with a complete understanding of who we are and how we're going to grow. Who else has God's vision? It's nice if people appreciate who we are and what we have done, but specifically seeking this from other people can turn us into slaves of their opinions. God accepts you, so that means you can accept you, too.

SPIRITUAL POSTURE 4 –

DETACHMENT

As discussed earlier, an attachment is a persistent demand our dysfunctional ego makes on us to satisfy a specific desire to the point that it becomes part of our identity. Attachments begin as desires and eventually grow into obsessions. The attachment may be to a particular career, title or position; it may be to one's wealth or social status; it could even be to another person. Each attachment leaves a psychological residue that uniquely reflects the nature of the ego's demand and degree to which it enshrouds the soul. For example, an attachment may ultimately cause a person to become irritable, paranoid, envious, worrisome, shameful or prejudiced, to name a few.

These ego residues are usually more visible to others than they are to the person with the attachments. This is because the ego is skilled at using defense mechanisms, such as denial or repression. It's not until the ego-possessed person awakens to his or her ego that the cost of having the attachment is realized. The truth of the matter is that for every attachment we have we pay a price in peace and happiness. Why? Because each attachment drains us of time, energy, money and relationships. At some point we finally say, "Enough is enough!" We begin to seek freedom from the prison that the attachments have built around us. When we realize this, spiritual posture 4 can be helpful.

Detaching does not mean we disassociate from people or things, but we begin to view them differently, in a way that brings greater respect and love to relationships with people and stewardship of things. As with taming our serpent ego, we cannot get rid of attachments through direct confrontation. Resistance and renunciation will not work. Judging them as bad or evil will not work. The ego is well-prepared for these tactics, and is a master at defeating them. So, a different approach is needed.

As with the ego, bringing attachments into the light of truth will begin to dissolve them. The two sides of this spiritual posture include seeing the attachment for what it really is, and feeling what life is really like without its burden. It feels good!

Begin by observing what the attachment really is and what it's really doing to us. See it for its cost, the suffering it brings. Attachments simply don't provide the value or the happiness the ego wants us to think they have. They can't sustain the happiness they promise. Attachments rob us of reality – of life itself. Our true happiness comes from within the soul, not from some external object, person or situation. The things of this world were given to us to care for and enjoy; they were not meant to possess us.

As we begin to shed the bonds of attachments, we will begin to feel life as it was meant to be. The feelings of inner peace and joy, however small at first, provide us with a sense of what life is really like without attachments. It is our natural condition, what God intended for us. Experiencing and remembering this sensation will help us to shed other attachments and keep us from developing new ones.

All physical things, including our bodies, are impermanent. As part of the physical world, they eventually change into something else. That is the nature of objects which are basically solid energy. Energy has to move, so it cannot remain confined in the boundaries of an object for long. But with this realization comes the understanding that there are parts of us that *are* permanent – our souls are pieces of God Himself, spirit matter, which are connected with Him now and forever. The breath of life comes from God and will return to God, but will always exist.

SPIRITUAL POSTURE 5 –

PRESENCE OF GOD

Spiritual posture 5, the presence of God, is learning to feel and see His presence in each and every moment of our lives. This is what we experienced in the garden of Eden, and this is what we can experience again with practice over time. When our egos flee from the light of truth we will have plenty of room for God once again. The gates to the Kingdom swing open.

> "Listen! I am standing at the door, knocking; if you hear my voice and open the door, I will come in to you and eat with you, and you with me." (Rev. 3:20)

The presence of God is the grace of God. Thomas Merton defines grace as "… the power and light of God in us, purifying our hearts, transforming us in Christ, making us true children of God, enabling us to act in the world as His instruments for good and His glory."[23] He goes on to say that the presence of the Holy Spirit within us changes us from carnal beings to spiritual beings.[24]

> "Do you not know that you are God's temple, and that God's Spirit dwells in you? … For God's temple is holy, and you are that temple." (I Corinthians 3:16)

God isn't someplace else in a far-off castle. He is right here with us; He is right here in us. " '…and they shall name him Emmanuel,' which means 'God is with us.' " (Matthew 1:23) But besides knowing that God is with us, that He is a part of us, it's still necessary to make a connection with Him in our life. How can we do this?

Much of the training and indoctrination we received as we went through life was based on concrete observations and thought. We were taught to see things for what they physically were: That thing you sit on is a chair; that flower is a plant; fire is combustion of materials; light is made up of photons racing through space; gravity holds things together. We were taught names and dates of things that happened in the past, and we were taught our multiplication tables. Much of what we were taught was based on our scientific understanding of the physical world, but we were also shaped by cultural norms that supported corporate profits and individual independence. This led us to a mentality of scarcity and materialism that made some rich and others poor. All of this cultural formation proved to be fertile ground for individual and collective egos, leaving little room for spiritual understanding and growth.

As the light of truth reenters our lives, the ego melts away taking with it the false principles and values that have served only a select few people to the detriment of others. We still know that that thing we sit on is a chair, but now we see it as a gift of God, something to rest on, something to use to sit down and talk with someone else, something to pull up to a table and share a meal with another person. We begin to look at people, things and our behavior much differently. As Aldous Huxley describes it:

> "The person who has learned to regard things as sacred symbols, persons as temples of the Holy Spirit, and actions as sacraments, is the person who has learned constantly to remind him/herself who they are, where they stand in relation to the universe and God, how they should behave toward their fellows and what they must do to come to their final end."[25]

When we allow the presence of God into our lives we begin to see things at an expanded level: We see things as being much more than their physical nature; we see people as much more than just another human being; we see our every movement as an act of God's love. This is how we connect with God; we let Him be in us and become us. Our eyes become His eyes, our hands become His hands, and our voice becomes His voice.

The tasks we do during the day, either as part of our occupation or household chores, become the means by which God moves among His people looking for ways to help and make the world better, even in the smallest of ways. It may be holding a door open for someone else, picking up an object off the street that may hurt someone else, or offering a smile to someone else in need of one. Making the day a little nicer for someone else is an act of great value to God. Man's world may put little value on these actions, but they warm the heart of God.

The voice of God speaks to each of us all day long. What does He sound like? He sounds like every person asking for help, or saying thanks, or offering a compliment. He is the sound of a child playing, every person laughing, every bird singing; He sounds like a busy city street or a symphony orchestra; we hear him in the hammering of a house being built, or in an ambulance siren; He's the sound of a clock ticking or a phone ringing; His voice is the sound of a storm wind or a gentle breeze. When you see a flower He is asking you to see more than just a plant – He is speaking, "See the beauty in the world? Share it and enjoy it!" God's voice is the sound of life, moment by moment.

So, if you're waiting for a message from God, He's waiting for you to hear the ones He's already sending you. Jean-Pierre de Caussade notes:

"You are seeking God and He is everywhere. Everything reveals Him to you, everything brings Him to you. He is by your side, over you, around and in you. Here is His dwelling and yet you still seek Him." [26]

Armed with these five spiritual postures, we're ready to explore our outer purpose – who we were made to be, and how we can serve Our Lord in our own unique way. Take your time on this spiritual journey. There is no rush. Be sure to allow yourself room for growing at your own pace. Be compassionate with yourself on your journey.

"This treasure of the Kingdom of God has been hidden by time and multiplicity and the soul's own works, or briefly by its creaturely nature. But in the measure that the soul can separate itself from this multiplicity, to that extent it reveals within itself the Kingdom of God. Here the soul and the Godhead are one."

Meister Eckhart

9 From Now On

"Do not be conformed to this world, but be transformed by the renewing of your minds, so that you may discern what is the will of God – what is good and acceptable and perfect."

(Romans 12:2)

"For surely you have heard about him and were taught in him, as truth is in Jesus. You were taught to put away your former way of life, your old self, corrupt and deluded by its lusts, and to be renewed in the spirit of your minds, and to clothe yourselves with the new self, created according to the likeness of God in true righteousness and holiness." (Ephesians 4:21-24)

Psalm 98 begins with a plea that we, as children of God, awaken to a new life: "O sing to the Lord a new song, for He has done marvelous things." When we awaken from the darkness that surrounds our soul, we become a new song in the heart of God. Our daily movements, thoughts and words become the spiritual notes we play on each measure of the day. Together we all are part of God's symphony of life; we are His instruments, each playing a part in His orchestra. Every thing we do and say sends out the sounds of love if we're in tune with Him. We learn whether it's our true selves doing the sweet singing, or if it's our off-key ego. As we shed the false self from our souls (like Paul did on the road to Damascus), the gifts of the Holy Spirit begin to flow through us out into the world in very special and unique ways depending on what gifts and talents each of us has been given. This is the new song!

YOUR OUTER PURPOSE

"So if anyone is in Christ, there is a new creation: everything old has passed away; see, everything has become new!" (2 Corinthians 5:17)

Besides our inner, primary purpose to awaken to God's love, we also have an outer, secondary purpose to our life. The outer purpose is how we actually live our life moment by moment once we have been freed from our dysfunctional ego. This outer purpose is how we actually express our uniqueness in serving God, serving others and ourselves as a co-creator with God. Contrary to what we may have been told by our parents, teachers, or the latest popular motivational speaker, we *cannot* become anything we want to be. Most of these 'wants' are a product of the ego, and as we have seen, the dysfunctional ego's primary interest is self-preservation and control. The only way we will ever be truly successful or happy is by being who God designed us to be in the first place. Ultimately, we can do nothing else. Living a lie will lead to a slow death spiritually and in many cases even physically (the body reacts negatively to the dissonance of the mind and soul).

When we have truly awakened, we will be able to get a much better look at the world around us. But more importantly, we'll gain a clearer understanding of who we are. We will know better the things we truly like to do and those we don't. Instead of asking "What do I want out of life?" we begin to ask "What does life want out of me?" and, "How can I use the special gifts, interests and talents that I have been given in service to others?"

It's true that we may still have to spend part of our day doing tasks that may not seem to fit who we really are so that we can provide for our basic needs. Often, however, we'll view even the most mundane tasks differently once we have a change in our awareness. We may come to realize that our mission in life may not be so much *what* we do as *how* we do it. We may come to realize that it's the people we interact with during these daily tasks that are the most important part of the day, and not the task itself. It may be a simple case of showing care and respect for the things we work with; a keyboard, a shovel, a drill, a hammer, or a plow. These are all gifts from God; they come from the earth, and deserve respect as though they are 'vessels of the altar.' The joy of the day will usually come from what we put into a task, not what we get out of it. Almost any constructive task done in the present moment can bring enjoyment.

> "Set your minds on things that are above, not on things that are on earth, for you have died, and your life is hidden with Christ in God. When Christ who is your life is revealed, then you also will be revealed with him in glory." (Colossians 3:2-4)

FORMATION

Spiritual formation is the process we use to strengthen and enrich our connections with God, with each other, and with nature once we awaken. To do this takes time. The process of "rewiring" our brains to conform to reality and our souls is an ongoing process –

remember that it took years for the ego to get where it is! Spiritual formation comes in many forms, depending on our personal situation and how we need to grow. We have seen how each person is made up of a mind, body and soul. These three interrelate within each of us in slightly different ways. Some people may be more body (service) oriented; others may be more soul (prayer) oriented; still others may be more mind (study) oriented. Each of the three components of a person (mind, body and soul) contributes a slightly different emphasis on our spiritual journey to God:

The way of devotion is related to the soul.
(Prayer orientation)
The way of knowledge is related to the mind.
(Study orientation)
The way of works is related to the body.
(Service orientation)

Most people have some combination of all three, but may still have a preference for one or the other. One way isn't better than the other, they are just different. So, as we work on our spiritual formation, we seek an agreeable blend of tools and techniques that best suits our temperament and interests. This will probably change over time. When we have established what works well for us, we may want to explore what some of the other methods have to offer. The ultimate end for any spiritual formation is union with God.

Formation is more often a process of removing things rather than one of adding new skills or behaviors. As we remove the false self that enshrouds our true self, the changes that happen to us are the result of the true self beginning to find its way to the surface. It's not really learning new behaviors; rather it's a matter of allowing natural behaviors to emerge. In the words of Anthony de Mello, our challenge is to recapture the simplicity and wisdom of the dove (the soul) without losing the cunningness of the brain. [27] Remember, the brain is a great tool. Although it's the source of the ego, it does not have to become dysfunctional. Formation is based on patience, observing, acceptance, and awareness – it isn't based on punishment and reward, discipline and control, sermonizing, ambition or guilt-based tactics.

Formation begins once we have awakened to the presence of the ego. The awareness of the ego and of the present moment is followed by acknowledgment of our situation. We strive to stay non-judgmental and non-resistant to each moment and what it brings. As we grow spiritually, ridding ourselves of the dysfunctional ego, the Holy Spirit flows more naturally through the soul and out into the world in very special and unique ways. This is the way life is supposed to be. This is enlightenment. This is the path to the gifts of the Holy Spirit – the peace, joy, patience, gentleness and love that is our own spiritual heritage. (Galatians 5:22) It's becoming and living who we were made to be – serving God in this world in our own unique way. Paul understood what this meant when he wrote to the Philippians:

> "Let the same mind be in you that was in Christ Jesus, who, though he was in the form of God, did not regard equality with God as something to be exploited, but he emptied himself, taking the form of a slave, being born in human likeness. And being found in human form, he humbled himself and became obedient to the point of death – even death on a cross." (Philippians 2:5-8)

Formation does not involve comparisons. It's not how we are doing in relation to another person (a system widely used in education and business today). Progress in formation is how you are doing in relation to yourself.

> "We do not dare to classify or compare ourselves with some of those who commend

151

themselves. But when they measure themselves by one another, and compare themselves with one another, they do not show good sense." (2 Corinthians 10:12)

In mankind's system, you will always be better than some people and inferior to others. There is an ordering or ranking that needs to be created for that system to work. But in God's system, when we get down to the essence of each person, you are neither superior nor inferior. You are just you.

"An artist is not a special kind of person, but every person is a special kind of artist." Ananda K. Coomaraswamy

Now let's explore each of the three ways of formation, keeping in mind that they are not mutually exclusive. There is no one right way for spiritual formation, and we will see that these three overlap each other and help each other in many ways.

THE WAY OF DEVOTION (The Soul)

The way of devotion involves activities related to spending time alone or with others in prayer, worship, meditation or contemplation. The importance of this type of life cannot be overstated. Some people devote their entire lives to prayer. Prayer is often thought of as speaking with God. Many people "say" prayers before meals, before going to bed at night, or during a church service. There are different styles of prayers, such as morning and evening prayer, holy readings (Lectio Divina), or the Rosary. Prayers can have different purposes, such as praise, thanksgiving, petitions for our self, intentions for others, or for inspiration.

Ultimately, prayer becomes a state of presence that we find ourselves in when we're fully connected with God. Our eyes become His eyes, our ears become His ears, and our hands become His hands. What we think, say and do become what He would think, say and do. It's at this point that we're praying continually. It's at this point that prayer becomes action – we begin to truly love God with all our heart and soul and strength, and we love our neighbors as our selves. This is one way that the way of devotion is linked to the way of works.

When the disciples asked Jesus how to pray, he taught them the Lord's Prayer. (Matthew 6:5-15) The very first words "Our Father" serves as a cornerstone for reconnecting with God. If He is our Father, then we are *all* His children. If we are all His children then we are all *one* family. Every man is our brother and every woman is our sister. This is truly a level playing field.

Jesus also demonstrated ways of praying. Sometimes it was in the presence of others, and sometimes it was alone. He used prayer to help others heal, to thank God for His mercy and compassion, and to seek God's support and guidance. Like Jesus, sometimes we pray alone, and sometimes with others. Sometimes we speak to God (or may even shout at Him) and other times we just listen. Sometimes prayer is simple silence, or a gentle walk in the woods (another example of how the way of devotion blends with the way of works). Other times it may involve hymns, incense, and bells. However we offer prayer, the main purpose is to bring our minds from the past or the future into the present moment where God can be found. We set aside the baggage of the past and the concerns of the future to reconnect with God in the only place we can find Him – in the here and now. William Law describes prayer:

> "Prayer is the nearest approach to God and the highest enjoyment of him that we are capable of in this life. It is the noblest exercise of the soul, the most exalted use of our best faculties,

and the highest imitation of the blessed inhabitants of Heaven."[28]

THE WAY OF KNOWLEDGE (The Mind)

The way of knowledge is the striving to know God through reason, experience and understanding. While the totality of God is beyond our comprehension, certain aspects of Him *are* knowable. When He planted His own image within each of us, He gave us a glimpse into His true and full nature that would serve as our guide and source of energy as we go through life.

The way of knowledge encourages us to add to our comprehension of the world around us. To know the world is to know something about God. To know what others wrote and thought about God is to know something about God. There are many things we can study for our continued spiritual growth. There are more books to read or classes to attend than we will ever have time for. Therefore we have to carefully discern the promptings of the Holy Spirit to determine which direction we need to pursue in the time that we have been given. Regardless of the topic or the place, however, the underlying purpose for our study is to move closer to becoming who we were truly meant to be. While part of this quest may be to hone a skill or learn a new topic, there is one area of study that ties in very closely with our awakening and present moment awareness. This is the study of our selves.

We return once again to the importance of observing our reactions to persons and situations as we move through time, moment by moment. With practice, we can begin to separate the observer from the observed. The observer is our true self, and the observed is the action that is happening in the moment. The action can be a thought, a movement, or a word. Initially, the reaction happens spontaneously, and we then have to stop and ask ourselves, why I thought what I thought, or why I said what I said, or why I did what I did. Was this action from the heart (the house of the soul) or from the head (the house of the ego)? Then ask, why did I react the way I did? Was it the ego just trying to protect itself? Or was it a true response from the heart? Review once again the five spiritual postures discussed earlier.

Remember also that engaging in contemplative experiences as done in the way of devotion will also teach you things about God. The way of devotion and the way of knowledge overlap when the experiences produced by prayer provide insights into the nature of God.

THE WAY OF WORKS (The Body)

The way of works is based on a special appreciation of our physical world and how it represents the creativity and love of God. It's being interactive with matter; it's finding fulfillment in creating, building, writing, walking, talking, organizing, and helping to name just a few. It's moving things, sharing things, growing things and building things so that greater equity is achieved among God's people through our hands.

The path to God through the way of works has many avenues. Some people connect with God when they write and play music. Others find God in care giving. Still others find Him by becoming the best athletes they can. The way of works is heavily rooted in present moment awareness because it deals extensively with the physical senses (touch, sight, hearing, smell and taste). People with a inclination to the way of works enjoy the sights and sounds of a prayer liturgy – the stain-glassed windows, the incense, the vestments, the hymns. Church services are places where the way of devotion and the way of works intersect. A walk in the woods can also be a prayer.

People following the way of works will often volunteer for projects that help others. They may help out at food pantries or assist in building or maintaining homes for those who need shelter. They may serve as teacher's aides or donate part of their day of work to helping others in a variety of ways.

Often overlooked is the job we have. We may not have thought about it as being a service to others, but if we think about it in broader terms we may realize that we are, in fact, helping God complete His plan. There is the story of the three masons working on a wall of a church. When asked what they were doing, one replied, "I'm stacking bricks on top of each other." The second replied, "I'm building a building." The third replied, "I'm creating a place where people can come to worship." Three people doing the same work, but each one doing a different job. Think about your job in new ways, with fresh imagination, and you may gain a greater appreciation for it.

COMMON THREADS

Regardless of which way of formation we prefer (or which combination of ways we use), each of the three paths has some common characteristics. Each path serves God by serving others in special ways.

"Like good stewards of the manifold grace of God, serve one another with whatever gift each of you has received." 1 Peter 4:10

Each way demonstrates charity to others. Charity is more than giving money to a worthy cause; it's giving of ourselves to the service of God. Jean Pierre Camus, a French bishop and writer of spiritual works, said, "Charity is the only virtue which unites us to God and man. Such union is our final aim and end, and all the rest is mere delusion." And, as we learned earlier, this all happens in the present moment. Charity isn't a thing of the past, or a hope of the future. As Aldous Huxley explains, it is *now*:

"The present moment is the only aperture through which the soul can pass out of time into eternity, through which grace can pass out of eternity into the soul, and through which charity can pass from one soul in time to another soul in time."[29]

Each of the three ways also leads us more toward a life of simplicity. Simplicity is responding to meet our true and natural needs (not our dysfunctional ego needs) with only what is necessary, and with the least impact on the world around us. Thus, we can make comparisons in our moment to moment choices: do I (the real "I") really need this thing, or is it a demand of the ego (the false "I")? And of the choices that fit these true needs, which is better for the environment? And, of the choices that I have, which adds greater beauty to the world? Thomas Merton describes simplicity:

> "Simplicity is the generous effort to sweep out of our lives all that is useless, all that is 'alien', all that is not willed for us by God."[30]

Aldous Huxley points out that when humility is perfect the most characteristic fruit is simplicity.[31] And, of course, simplicity isn't just measured by the amount of things, but it's also a state of being as Fénelon states, "That soul which looks where it is going without losing time arguing over every step, or looking back perpetually, possesses true simplicity."

Let's not forget about our health, too. The body is the container for our soul and it will serve us best if it's being served properly. We become more effective at prayer, study and service if we treat our body in the way that it was meant to be treated – as a temple of the Holy Spirit. We often push ourselves beyond what we were designed to be able to do mentally and physically. This is often a product of the dysfunctional ego that pushes us to achieve unnatural levels of performance or endurance to reach a set of unrealistic standards that were set by cultural norms. The phrase 24/7 is now a standard part of our lifestyle. We have left almost no margin in our life. We often ignore God's guidance that we rest one day out of seven. He thought it was important enough to make it a commandment!

Not only is getting enough rest a challenge in today's world, but nutrition and personal image are also being manipulated by collective corporate egos. On the one hand, because there is profit in consumption, we have been seduced by corporate programming into eating foods that disrupt our bodily processes. On the other hand, we have been seduced into false standards of surface beauty so that we pour billions of dollars into cosmetics, exercise equipment and unnecessary plastic surgery. They have been trying to convince us that physical appearance is all that matters. So, one industry makes money fattening us up by having us eat too much, and another industry makes money by trying to trim us down. Our dysfunctional egos will play right into their hands. A perfect trap!

> "Our whole business in this life is to restore
> to health the eye of the heart whereby God may
> be seen." St. Augustine

When we learn the truth about the body we will not be eating unnatural foods, or stressing ourselves beyond how we were designed. We will learn where true beauty is found, and we will understand our true place in nature. We have limitations as humans, and rather than ignore them or label them as weaknesses, we would do better by leveraging them together as a community. Our limitations as individuals are what can bring us together as a family.

WALK WITH OTHERS

> "If you want to go fast, go alone. If you want
> to go far, go together." African Proverb

The need for community, to be with other people of like mind and purpose, stems from two sources. First, it comes from our physical nature. This has sometimes been referred to as "herd instinct." To survive and prosper in the physical world, there are advantages to being with others such as added protection and the sharing of resources. Creatures that operate alone, who are disconnected from others, are at risk in nature. So, it's often better to be in a group of friends and allies if threatened. There is some truth to the saying that there is safety in numbers.

> "Two are better than one, because they have a good reward for their toil. For if they fall, one will lift up the other; but woe to the one who is alone and falls and does not have the other to help." (Ecclesiastes 4:9-10)

The other need for community comes from the soul. The desire to be with other people stems from the fact that we're all connected spiritually. Since God put His image into each one of us through the breath of life, we are connected to Him, to every other person, and to nature itself. We are all one in this sense. Being connected in this way creates a natural inclination to interact and be near others who realize this connection. This becomes easiest and most enjoyable if we connect with others on a soul-to-soul level.

It's therefore wise to surround yourself with a team that supports your spiritual journey. Set boundaries with those who may be toxic to you; people who are operating from their dysfunctional ego and are simply out to use you for their own ego survival and growth. Find people who are soul-driven, those who are interested in helping you become who you were meant to be. This is love. These people can be friends, spiritual advisors, mentors, counselors, therapists, teachers, and guides. It may take time to find the right people, but it's well worth it. And don't forget to stay connected with the Holy Spirit, because the Holy Spirit is your teacher. (John 14:26)

SUMMARY

Formation brings us freedom. This freedom isn't simply the ability to choose between good and evil, but rather it's the freedom of growing into a true preference for good over evil. If we consider all the people of the world as the unitive body of Christ, then we can imagine that this body will only be truly healthy when all of its parts are awake and functioning properly. Perhaps it's true on a global scale what St. Paul writes, "If one member suffers, all suffer together with it…" (I

Corinthians 12:26) We are more connected with each other and the world than we think we are. What we need is very near to us; it's not something that is hard to obtain.

"Surely, this commandment that I am commanding you today is not too hard for you, nor is it too far away. It is not in heaven, that you should say, 'Who will go up to heaven for us, and get it for us so that we may hear it and observe it?' Neither is it beyond the sea, that you should say, 'Who will cross to the other side of the sea for us, and get it for us so that we may hear it and observe it?' No, the word is very near to you; it is in your mouth and in your heart for you to observe." (Deut. 30:11-14)

Are the words that Moses spoke to the people in Deuteronomy 30 applicable to us today? He advises, "If you return to the Lord your God, and you and your children obey Him with all your heart and with all your soul, just as I am commanding you today, then the Lord God will restore your fortunes and have compassion on you..." What would happen if *all* the people of the world woke up to their soul and began living their own true purpose in life, loving God with all their heart, and with all their soul, and with all their might; and loving their neighbors and themselves? How much pain and suffering would we eliminate in the world? How much more of God's abundance would we enjoy?

We will reclaim Eden if we fully awaken to the image of God that was given to each of us. Finding this image will lead us once again to the community of God, to the richness of His mercy and compassion, and to the life He meant us to have.

ENDNOTES

1. Stephen H. Webb, *In Whose Image? The meaning of the imago Dei* (Christianity Today International, July/August 2006, Vol. 12, No. 4), p. 10.

2. Robert Alter, *Genesis: Translation and Commentary* (Norton Publishing, New York, 1996).

3. Aldous Huxley, *The Perennial Philosophy: An Interpretation of the Great Mystics, East and West* (Harper-Collins, 2004), p. 140.

4. Thomas Merton, *Life and Holiness* (Image Books, New York, 1969) p. 12.

5. Aldous Huxley, *The Perennial Philosophy*, p. 165.

6. Robert Alter, *Genesis: Translation and Commentary*, p. 9.

7. Aldous Huxley, *The Perennial Philosophy*, p. 213.

8. Ephraim A. Speiser, *The Anchor Bible, Genesis: A New Translation with Introduction and Commentary* (Doubleday & Co., New York, 1964), p. 20.

9. Albertus Pieters, *Notes on Genesis: Old Testament History – Volume I* (Eerdmans Publishing Company, Grand Rapids, MI, 1954), p. 81.

10. Ibid. p. 81.

11. Gregory A. Boyd, *Repenting of Religion: Turning from Judgment to the Love of God* (Baker Books, Grand Rapids, 2004), p. 77.

12. Ibid. p. 79.

13. Robert Alter, *Genesis: Translation and Commentary*, p. 11.

14. Aldous Huxley, *The Perennial Philosophy*, p. 272.

15. Thomas Merton, *The Silent Life* (Noonday Press, New York, 1957), p. 15.

16. Gregory of Nyssa, Beatitudes, Sermon 8.

17. Thomas Hardy, *Tess of the D'Urbervilles* (Penguin, New York, 1998), p. 114.

18. Irenaeus of Lyons, *Against Heresies*, III, 23.6.

19. Gregory Nazianzen, *Oration 45,* For Easter, 8.

20. Eckhart Tolle, *The New Earth: Awakening to Your Life's Purpose* (Penguin, New York, 2005), p. 14.

21. Eckhart Tolle, *Power of Now: A Guide to Spiritual Enlightenment* (New World Library, CA., 1999), p. 21.

22. Anthony de Mello, *The Way to Love*, (Doubleday, New York, 1991), p. 162.

23. Thomas Merton, *Life and Holiness*, p. 7.

24. Ibid. p. 30.

25. Aldous Huxley, *The Perennial Philosophy*, p. 271.

26. Jean-Pierre de Caussade, *Sacrament of the Present Moment,* (Harper San Francisco, 1966), p. 18.

27. Anthony de Mello, *The Way to Love*, p. 75-79.

28. William Law, *A Serious Call to a Devout and Holy Life,* (Harper San Francisco, 1978), p. 46.

29. Aldous Huxley, *The Perennial Philosophy*, p. 188.

30. Thomas Merton, *The Silent Life*, p. 22.

31. Aldous Huxley, *The Perennial Philosophy*, p. 112.

LaVergne, TN USA
14 November 2009
164166LV00002B/13/P